To Barbara,
with lots of wor[?] [?] [?] is
memories over the [?] is
My best,

Stanley

12/8/99

THANK MY LUCKY STARS

A MEMOIR OF A
GLAMOROUS ERA
STANLEY PAUL

as told to Diane Palmer

KENDALL/HUNT PUBLISHING COMPANY
4050 Westmark Drive   Dubuque, Iowa 52002

I dedicate this book to all
the people who have touched
my life in Chicago—

My kind of town

Copyright © 1999 by Stanley Paul and Diane Palmer

Library of Congress Catalog Card Number: 99-73290

ISBN 0-7872-5770-2

Kendall/Hunt Publishing Company has the exclusive rights to reproduce this work,
to prepare derivative works from this work, to publicly distribute this work,
to publicly perform this work and to publicly display this work.

Printed in the United States of America
10 9 8 7 6 5 4 3 2 1

CONTENTS

On the 12th of May in 1973, I was where I'd been for the better part of the last ten years . . . at the Pump Room in Chicago's Ambassador East Hotel. It was a typical Saturday night, nearly half past nine, in what had become one of the world's most famous rooms. Where celebrities mingled with socialites. Where people came to see and be seen. Red-coated waiters carrying swords skewered with flaming food were everywhere, and the dance floor was crowded with tuxedoed forms pressed against gowns. And tonight, every table was taken. Every booth was filled. . . except one, that open booth so conspicuously vacant in the otherwise crowded room. It was Booth One, the booth reserved for the famous . . . and it was waiting.

I was at my usual place, sitting at the piano on the bandstand, leading my orchestra from the far left corner of the crowded room. And the dull roar of conversation blended in with the music—and the wagons, clamoring through the aisles carrying salads, flaming desserts and copper chafing dishes. If all those swords and desserts served that night had arrived at the same time, the second Chicago fire would have been a definite possibility.

I could see everything from my position: the diners, the dancers, and the entrance . . . *filled with clouds of smoke I suddenly noticed!* And then, the deep throated shriek that could mean only one thing. She was here!

Standing there in the entrance, with one arm on her hip and the other waving a cigarette madly in the air, she commanded the attention of the room as everyone paused to stare at her. "But I've al-rea-dy *told* you . . . I don't *want* to be seated in Booth One!" she said so *loudly*, each syllable spit out like a bullet in some subdued rapid fire. "I will be sit-ting with Stanleypaul at the pi-a-no!" She'd always pronounced my name as though it were one word, and my smile turned to a grin as we launched into *Too Marvelous for Words.*

"But, Miss Davis," the maître d' began to explain, "you will be more comfortable in Booth One." He was only attempting to put everything in order. As the reigning celebrity in the Pump Room that night, and any other night she was there, Bette Davis was entitled to sit in the booth closest to the entrance, and farthest from the bandstand.

"Jeeez!" . . . the voice again, but quieter now. The room was silent.

She brought her cigarette back up to her mouth, inhaled, exhaled and turned in one swift movement, then moved like a tidal wave right through the entrance and across the thickly carpeted floor. I had to admit, she was still the queen of dramatic entrances. Conversation had stopped completely and it was just the music . . . and the wagons, which had slowed to a quiet roll. The room seemed in slow motion as she approached the stage, people quietly scrambling to get out of her way. And then the murmur began, a thousand whispers coming from heads attached to out-stretched necks trying to catch a glimpse of the Hollywood legend.

"My *Gawd* there hhyou are!" she called out to me, breathing through a word now and then as only Bette Davis ever did. "What an ex-*traaa*-va-gant bas-ket was wai-ting in my suite u-pon my a-hhrri-val. You must *reeea*-lly be do-ing well!"

I'd had a basket of fruit, cheeses and a bottle of scotch sent up to her suite before she'd checked

"Where did you get those awful sideburns?"

in. From what I could see I guessed she'd sampled at least the liquid portion of the gift. She hoisted herself up onto the bandstand, with the timely assistance of the bass player, and slid herself onto the piano bench beside me.

"Where did you *e*-vah get those aw-ful *side* burns?" she laughed, nearly pushing me right off the edge of the bench, as the smirk that had become her signature expression seemed to turn itself toward a smile, then back again. "Wai-tah!" she cried, turning her gaze back out toward the dance floor, as couples still stared up at us, nearly motionless. "*Brihhhing* me a scotch!"

She opened her handbag and took out a crimson red lipstick, smeared it across her top and bottom lip in one fluid motion, put it back in her bag and took out a pack of cigarettes. She removed one and set the pack up beside the ashtray. Then she took out a lighter, shut the bag, brought the cigarette to her mouth and lit it, exhaling every bit of smoke she'd just inhaled. Such an ordinary series of motions, but when she did them they took on a profound sense of the dramatic. A masterful performance.

"Such *mem*-ries you are bring-ing me with this mu-sic." she said, and then without warning, burst into song, if you could call it that. Singing in key was one performance skill she lacked. But her audience was riveted to her anyway.

The waiter arrived with her scotch and she stopped singing long enough to take a drink, then set it down on the piano and picked up where she'd left off. Unfortunately, however, the orchestra hadn't, and before the words and the music got too horribly out of sync, I signaled that we switch to *Red Roses for a Blue Lady*, her favorite.

"My *Gawd!* My *youuuth!*" she cried and burst into song again. The room relaxed. Diners went back to their meals, dancers returned to their dance. And meanwhile, I was restricting my playing to just the middle keys to keep from knocking her off of the piano bench, all the while envisioning tomorrow's headlines:

BETTE DAVIS FLOORED BY PIANO PLAYER

Stanley Paul Offers Thousand Apologies

NOT ACCEPTED

An hour passed without our ever taking a break. A thick cloud of smoke had settled in around us long ago, two ashtrays completely filled. And the orchestra members kept glaring at me, more than anxious to stop for their long past scheduled break. But our guest of honor had no interest in stopping, no interest whatsoever. And none of us, least of all me, was remotely inclined to disappoint her.

We were playing *I Only Have Eyes for You,* and I started to sing along with her as she bellowed on, completely off key. In music, there are only the keys of A through G. Bette Davis spent the evening singing in the key of H—whatever the Hell key she wanted.

She lifted her continuously refilled glass of scotch from its place on the piano, took a drink, stared at me awhile as though about to speak, then put it down. Then she turned and leaned in closer, lowering her voice so that only the orchestra and the dancers within a hundred feet of the bandstand could hear. "You must *not* sing Stanleypaul. Nev-ah, *e*-vah sing, Stanleypaul. You do re-*mem*-ber that?" she pronounced much more than she asked.

My first thought was, "Talk about the pot calling the kettle black!" but of course, she was right. Singing was neither of our strong suits. "All right! No argument here!" I laughed.

She threw her head back then and started the low sort of growling laugh that she had, raised her head then her throaty voice and shouted, volume building, "Now . . . you just *play! Start* at the be-gin-ning, Stanleypaul."

"The beginning." I thought as I started to play . . . remembering.

CHAPTER ONE

BEGINNINGS

I declared myself a professional musician and moved to New York in the summer of 1960, just after college graduation from Penn State. I'd majored in music education, but never had any interest in educating anyone other than myself. I was just there to make good on a promise, all the while just hoping and planning for something else. Planning for the real beginning of my life.

After my father died, it was my mother who'd insisted I get a degree when I'd declared my intention to come to New York City. She became much more security oriented than she'd been while he was alive. Since my sister, Raelene, had married by then, I was the only child left to worry about. I'd always talked about becoming a musician, but my mother never really took it seriously. She hoped I'd pick up where my father left off, running what she continually reminded me was "the most successful men's clothing store in West Chester, Pennsylvania."

I grew up in West Chester, Pennsylvania. It was a small town, of no more than 13,000 people, where most everyone knew most everyone else. When you walked down the street people asked how you were doing. They inquired about your day. Your life. Your family. It was a comfortable place. No surprises. No real high points once you attended the Senior Prom and got married. No low points that weren't expected in life.

"New York!" she'd exclaimed the day I shared my plan with my mother. "Just what that city needs—another piano player!"

There was no question by that point that I had musical talent, something that was discovered when I was almost four years old. That was when

My mother, my sister and the six-month-old pianist to be.

my parents found me hammering out the Lone Ranger theme on the keys of our piano as The Masked Man, his great horse Silver and Tonto rode through the dust over the waves blasting from our upright radio. Both my parents were thrilled, and that very afternoon I was rushed off to a piano teacher where my classical training started. They strapped big blocks of wood to the pedals so my legs could reach them. It was clear from the start that I didn't really fit the 'classical musician' image. I was always a small show stopper, a born comedian when I was supposed to be most serious.

After only a few weeks of lessons, my mother announced that I was going to be "*on the radio,*" on a 'Kiddie Show' being broadcast from Philadelphia, the big city. I kept trying to imagine what it would be like. Then one day, while my parents were out of the house, I actually pulled our big, wooden upright Zenith radio, a clunky piece of furniture, out from against the wall. It took all my strength to inch it forward, then I squeezed myself into the space behind it while it was playing. I just stood there, looking at all those tubes glowing, trying to figure out how people got in them and,

I was a born ham.

even more important, how they got out. I was scared to death!

I was crying when they found me a little later, wailing, "I'm too big to be on the radio!" I had pulled all the tubes from their sockets so there'd be room for me to fit inside of the box. My parents were in stitches and my sister never let me forget! For years, she'd walk through the house saying, "Where's Stanley? Is he stuck in that radio again?"

Music had always been a big part of my family's life. Our parents had purchased a piano not long after they married, hoping that one of their children might eventually "demonstrate an aptitude" for it. But my older sister, Raelene, hadn't the slightest interest in music. Like my mother, she was more focused on keeping her dolls in the latest styles of women's fashions. That would later lead to a successful modeling career. By the time my mother became pregnant with me, out of desperation to have someone use the piano that became a silent piece of furniture in the living room, she'd started taking piano lessons herself.

"Miriam, it's amazing . . ." my father would often remark. "You took lessons twice a week, practiced every day for nine months, and never did learn to play one damn song yourself. But by God, at least someone benefited from all that work!"

"That's right Joe . . ." she'd always respond, smiling back at him proudly.

I was the one who'd developed a passion for music, as though I'd been predestined for it. My parents gave me their wholehearted support. Even on nights my parents went out with friends, we spent at least some part of the evening around the piano in the living room. They'd sing while I played, and sometimes my father would tell us stories about all the performers he saw in Vaudeville when he was young. Names like Al Jolson, Eddie Canter and Sophie Tucker. I'd just play along to the melodies he'd sing out, learning the songs and singing along with everyone else. Looking back on it now, I think a good part of the fascination I've always had with old songs and old performers had its beginnings with the fun we used to have around that piano.

My father, as a young man, never missed a vaudeville show in Philadelphia.

My father put his heart and soul into his business. My mother not only raised two children, but was always going to one meeting or another, raising money for a worthy cause or contributing to the advancement of some educational endeavor, and making sure she looked great doing it! They both maintained a very social existence as community leaders. Their values, like their lifestyle, couldn't help but rub off on their children—not if they had anything to say about it.

I'd always had a lot of friends, in spite of the fact that I had to practice for hours each day after school. One of our housekeeper's duties was to keep tabs on my progress which, as luck would have it, she did from the kitchen. As long as she heard what she thought was classical music coming out of the piano, she'd proudly report to my parents that I'd been doing just what they'd instructed. Unbeknownst to her, half the time I'd be reading comic books while I was practicing,

Maybe that's why I can still carry on a conversation while I play, and stay focused on both.

One of my earliest memories involves trying to run a men's store of my own right in front of my father's. I wasn't even in kindergarten when I set up an orange crate and stood behind it selling ties that I'd found in an old box on our front stairs that morning. My mother had set them out for pick up by the Salvation Army. As far as I was concerned, they represented an irresistible business opportunity. I offered them for sale at a huge discount compared to my father's prices. I sold the ties until my father discovered what I was up to and put an end to it. He was proud of me, he said, and gave me a quarter for my inventiveness. He also explained that in order to sell something I had to own it first!

After that, I sold anything and everything but clothing from behind that orange crate in front of my father's store. At first I made things—works of art, I called them. Then I'd buy things and resell them at a profit.

I got my picture in the paper as a five year old who'd managed to sell $25 worth of war stamps. But before long I stopped *spending* my allowance, and started investing it in things I'd find at flea markets or in thrift shops. I'd clean them up a little or make a minor repair here or there, then sell them for three to five times what I paid for them. Eventually I wound up convincing the local barber that his store front window could be put to better use, displayed some of my better finds there and gave him a small percentage of everything I made. People were calling me enterprising. I was learning that resourcefulness is what saves you when talent isn't enough.

I've never been shy, and even as a kid I came to life in a spotlight, especially playing music! Any time there was an opportunity to play something in public I took it, but as long as my parents were within earshot, the opportunities to play anything wilder than the classics were few and far between.

When I was about ten years old, my aunt and uncle came to visit with us at our summer place in Atlantic City. They spent the better part of a day taking me to the Boardwalk and looking at the sights. I even had my picture taken in a huge toy airplane.

Late in the afternoon we stopped into a club just off the boardwalk so they could make a telephone call. While I was waiting for them I spotted the piano. It was on an elevated platform in the center of the bar, and no one was playing it so I climbed up and started.

After the first few tunes came clamoring out, people started gathering around, making requests, and throwing change down onto the floor around me. For the next half hour I was in heaven, grinning as usual, and even my aunt and uncle were enjoying the show. But we made a pact to make no mention of the whole experience to my parents because we were certain that they wouldn't appreciate the idea of their little 10-year-old entertaining in a saloon. And it was a pact we kept, too.

I snuck away the next day, though, running along the beach as fast as I could and finding my way back to the same club. The owners were nice to me, but explained that I couldn't play there again. I was much too young, but I could come back in a few years when I was twenty-one. A lifetime away for me. I was crushed. I'd gotten a taste of what it felt like to play that music the way I played it. And from that point forward, it was everything I wanted.

My next big opportunity came when I was sixteen years old and had been playing with a combo on Saturday nights at a VFW hall just around the corner from my father's store for two years. My parents had no real objections since they knew most of the lodge members who assured them I'd be served no alcohol and be home by 11 p.m. And the eight to ten dollars a night I earned could be put toward adding to the model railroad I was building.

One of the guys in the combo told me that he'd heard that a bar owner in Philadelphia needed someone to play Debussy's *Claire du Lune* for a dancer named Sally Rand. They were offering thirty dollars a night. Since I was the only one in the group who played classical music, he thought I might be interested. I'd never heard of Sally Rand, but thirty dollars! Of course I was interested! The problem was that you had to be twenty-one to even drink in Pennsylvania let alone play piano in a bar. While I considered myself a very mature sixteen, I looked so much younger that even the local police pulled me over on occasion to show them some ID when I'd drive the second-hand car my parents had given me for my sixteenth birthday! All I could think about was, "Thirty dollars! And the chance to play in a big city like Philadelphia!"

The temptation was overwhelming. Then I had an idea. If I had gray hair and wore sunglasses, who would know that I was really only 16? So my friend called the club owner, settled the deal and the next thing I knew I was on my way. My parents had gone to a wedding that evening, thank God, and had no idea I'd be driving twenty-five miles alone in a car all the way to Philadelphia. They also never discovered that I'd bought a bottle of white shoe polish and smeared it through my hair to make myself look older. All the way there in the car I was practicing lowering my voice and looking stern so everyone would think that I was a mature pianist. I hoped my voice wouldn't crack as I said, "How . . . do . . . you . . . do? I am the person known as Stanley Paul, the pianist who plays Debussy."

Though I lost my way a few times, I finally pulled up to the place about an hour later. The sign outside the club announced that "The Legendary Sally Rand" would be appearing that evening. As I put on my sunglasses I kept wondering just what kind of dancer she was. I assumed it was ballet, since I'd played for practicing students on Saturday afternoons at Elsie Slider's Dance Studio in West Chester and I couldn't imagine anyone doing tap to Debussy.

As I walked into darkness and the smell of smoke and stale beer, scared to death of discovery but trying hard to hide it, I realized that I was going to work in a dive.

"I'm the p-p-piano player for Miss Rand," I said to the first person I saw. Without saying a word, he just pointed toward this little stage off in the corner. I thought, "So far, so good."

Just behind the postage-stamp-size stage, I saw a drum set and an old beat up upright piano. Since no one was around I sat down and started to practice my song. "Boy is this out of tune!" I thought.

A few minutes later this lady wearing a kimono appeared. "Honey, just keep it in tempo for the whole song," she whispered. Then she disappeared. From the looks of her I figured she was probably the dancer's mother.

About half an hour later a guy sat down at the drum set, someone else sauntered in with a saxo-phone and an old man practically shoved me off the bench as he sat down. "Go stand over there." he pointed.

As I took my place on the sidelines, the band started playing a brassy melody. A buxom woman walked onto the stage and started what she seemed to think was singing. After a few songs, the band disappeared and a comedian started telling dirty jokes. While I was busy trying to remember the punch lines so I could share them with the guys at school, I heard someone announce, "And *now* . . . in *person* . . . the *legend herself* . . . Miss *Sally* . . . *Rand!*"

I scrambled back onto the piano bench and out comes this little lady with these two enormous fans. It's the same woman that I thought was the dancer's mother!

She gave me the signal to start. After performing the first few bars of *Claire du Lune*, I looked up and saw that she was waving the fans around. "My *God!*" I realized. "She's not wearing any *clothes*!"

From my vantage point I could see *much* more than the audience could and the song sort of played itself while my eyes stayed riveted to this spectacle before me. "She's older than my mother!" kept screaming through my thoughts, and I had never seen my mother like that!

Sweat was pouring from my body by the time it was over. But that was only the first act. About an hour later, after the singer vocalized the same songs and the comedian did the same jokes, the legend herself reappeared. I was more relaxed by now until I realized that it was after midnight. I kept thinking, "My parents are gonna kill me!"

After the second show, I went up to the cash register and asked the owner for my money. He took one look at me and his mouth dropped open. "Jesus *Christ*! Are you nuts! How old are you anyway?" he said, and before I could answer he shoved some bills in my hand and screamed "Get the hell out of here! Ya wanna close up the joint?"

I cleared out as fast as I could and scrambled into the car, started the engine and drove off. The words *"My parents are gonna kill me!"* kept repeating themselves over and over in my head. I never had an opportunity to count the money until I got to the first stop light, where I discovered that all that was there was twenty bucks! I couldn't believe it! They cheated me out of ten dollars! I considered turning the car around, marching in and demanding the rest of the money, but when the light turned green I just kept going. It was late, I was tired and, if the truth be known, I was too scared to face that club owner again. I had enough to worry about just having to face my parents.

"They're probably asleep by now," I started convincing myself as I drove on. "Maybe they never even noticed I was missing!"

It was well after 2 a.m. when I pulled up in front of the house. "Where *were* you?" both of them screamed, running down the stairs to meet me. "We were ready to call the police!"

I told them the whole story, as best I could under the circumstances. After I finished, my mother warned, "You're going to ruin your life if you keep this up!" They were words I'd come to hear often in coming years.

Then, rather than being angry at me, they seemed amazed that I had actually played for Sally Rand. "We saw her in Chicago . . . at the World's Fair, didn't we, Joe?" my mother said. "And that was . . . when? Right after we were married in 1933!"

"She can't still be dancing over twenty years later!" my father answered. "I wonder what that woman looks like without her clothes."

"Joe," my mother said, using her warning tone of voice, "you should live so long."

The two of them went to bed, just shaking their heads. Somehow, the amazement that Sally Rand was still doing her fan dance at her advanced

"And I had never seen my mother like that!"   (Corbis/Bettmann)

age had caused them to forget to punish me for coming in over three hours past my curfew.

Had I pursued a more traditional career as a classical pianist, my family would have supported it wholeheartedly. As it was, they'd nurtured my talent since it was discovered, giving me every opportunity to develop, sparing no effort or expense to provide the tools I needed. But though I'd studied the works of the masters, the profession I'd opted for was far from the one they'd imagined. I didn't want to be alone on a stage in a concert hall, I wanted to be where *life* was I wanted to play in the clubs! And that was much too risky. It was fiscal foolishness as far as my parents were concerned.

My mother and I made a deal after my father's death. If I was going to pursue a dream with such an incredible risk of failure, she'd approve on the condition I agree to earn a degree, as something to "fall back on" in the event of total failure. She did have a point. There *were* a thousand piano players in New York. But not like *me*, I was convinced. And in 1960, equipped with a degree and an I.D. that entitled me to drink, the time had come to prove it.

But there was another motivating force. Pressure was mounting to take on the family business. I could go to New York and try my luck without opposition only because of a promise to my mother. If it didn't work out, I'd come back and become a haberdasher. A fate worse than death as far as I was concerned. In more ways than one, it was now or never.

CHAPTER TWO

STARTING OUT

Determined to succeed without financial assistance from my family, I arrived in New York with $800 to my name, money I'd earned in college playing occasional gigs with bands made up of my fraternity brothers. One of them had left school early and moved into a small rent controlled apartment on West 13th Street in Greenwich Village. He hadn't been successful finding work, so by the time I'd arrived his funds were running low and he needed a roommate to split the rent. I accepted immediately, and the next day started looking for work myself.

The first step was a trip to the Musicians' Union on West 52nd Street to register. They asked for some proof that I'd been a New York resident for at least six months. "Ugh oh . . ." I thought to myself and told them I'd be back with what they needed in a few hours. I walked back to my new apartment trying to figure out a way to prove I'd been living here all those months that I wasn't.

My roommate came up with the answer. He had utility bills and all sorts of mail that had been sent to him at the New York address. All we had to do was change the name from his to mine, which was accomplished with an eraser, a sheet of carbon paper and a typewriter. Three hours later I was leaving the Musicians' Union again, having successfully completed my registration.

Other than my roommate, I had only one contact in New York, a woman who owned a club in the Village called the Versailles. Those days there seemed to be a piano bar on every corner in New York, but this club was much more sophisticated. One of my fraternity brothers had told me the owner, Trude Heller, hired only the best musicians and had her pick of the lot thanks to the club's reputation. Once she heard me, he predicted, I'd be "hired in a minute."

I went to see Trude Heller late in the afternoon, an hour or so after the club opened. She was sitting at the end of the bar, going through a stack of receipts and punching numbers into one of those old fashioned adding machines, the kind with the handle sticking out of the side that worked like a crank.

"Trude?" I asked as I walked through the door, smiling and trying to look as confident as possible. She was a thin, rather elegant looking woman who gave me the a quick once over. I was frozen before she even spoke.

"It's *Mrs.* Heller and if you're going to be drinking I'll need to see some I.D." She spoke slowly and glared at me. I hadn't even introduced myself and the conversation seemed to be nearly concluded.

"Oh no! I'm not drinking," I beamed back at her. "And the only thing I'm selling is *me*," I added. "I play piano . . . quite well actually, and if you need someone I could really use a job."

She said nothing at first, just kept looking at me. "I'm pretty good . . . really." I said almost repeating myself, needing to somehow fill the silence. "I'll show you!" and then I turned and started toward the piano.

"Hold it right there," she called out after me, freezing me there in my tracks. "Turn around," she said.

As I spun around quickly to face her, she challenged, "You think you can just waltz into a place like mine, sit down at my piano and take up my time? You've never worked anywhere in this city, have you?"

"Well, no." I said nervously. "But I'm new to New York. I've just arrived. A friend of mine gave me your . . ."

"This is not a kindergarten class," she cut me off in mid-sentence. "There are hundreds of experienced piano players in New York looking for work. I'm not interested in children. Now get out," she dismissed me. She started cranking the adding machine again.

I was stunned as I turned and shuffled myself out the door. I felt small, foolish and very young. My mother's warnings echoed over and over in my head. My mother and Mrs. Heller used virtually the same words when talking about my career!

"Some start *that* was," I thought to myself. But I wasn't about to give up after one bad experience with some shortsighted woman who hadn't even heard me play! Once I got someone to hear me, I was sure I'd be on my way. But how? I needed a plan, a gimmick of some sort. But what?

I went back to our apartment, took out the Yellow Pages, and started cold calling night clubs that same afternoon. I asked to speak to the owner. Half of them weren't there, and the ones I spoke to asked for references, the name of my agent, places I'd played. And when I started to explain that I was new to New York, looking for my first job, they either just laughed at me or hung up.

That night I went to a few of the clubs I'd called to scope out the competition. I met a few musicians, and by the end of the night I'd learned a lot. Getting an agent, I was told, was a first step.

The next morning, I pulled out the now familiar Yellow Pages again and started calling theatrical agents. The listings went on for pages, and there was no way to tell who was good from who wasn't. Just one name after another, and there were hundreds! I called them all one by one, and usually never got past the secretary, who always said, "Send a photo and a list of where you've appeared. We'll keep it on file and give you a call." They all pretty much guaranteed the same thing, although I knew it was a fast way of ending the phone call.

Others asked where I was appearing now and offered to come hear me play sometime. Just like the club owners, no one was interested once I explained that I hadn't gotten my first job yet. I even suggested I come in and play for them, but no one wanted any part of that. If I didn't have a job, they weren't interested. And I couldn't get a job unless I played somewhere else first.

Then, one of my new found friends told me about an agent who booked a lot of the chic little supper clubs on the east side of New York, just the kinds of clubs I'd dreamt about. He'd just gotten a job for a "brilliant" pianist named Bernie Niero, who would soon be known as Peter Nero, at a club called Jilly's on West 52nd Street. "That could be me!" I kept thinking, "If I could just get him to hear me!"

The agent's name was Henry Hermann, but it was impossible for an inexperienced musician to get an appointment with him. I called anyway and heard his secretary start the standard "send a photo, tell us where your are playing" speech. I'd heard those lines a thousand times by now and simply hung up.

"How did anyone ever get a job in the first place?" I asked myself, and then from nowhere I got an idea! I started rehearsing, practicing conversations and changing the tone of my voice so as not to be recognized. I called Mr. Hermann back an hour later.

"Good morning," I responded to the secretary's greeting. "May I speak with Mr. Hermann please?"

"Whom may I say is calling?" she asked politely.

"Just tell him it's Stanley Paul. I've a business proposition to discuss with him involving a club," I said. Then I just held my breath. I didn't say I played the piano or that I was even looking for a job. Moments passed like hours and the phone was getting so wet it almost slipped from the now trembling hand that held it, and then he was on the phone.

"This is Henry Hermann." he answered, then waited for my explanation.

"Mr. Hermann, my name is Stanley Paul." I spoke the words slowly, clearly, trying to sound as much like a fifty year old business man as I could. "I really need some help with a night club deal, but if you don't mind I'd rather not get into the details over the phone. We could discuss it over lunch . . ." I suggested. "I can meet you at 21 any day this week if you're free," I added, hoping to impress him by inviting him to a swanky, expensive place. And a few minutes later we actually had a date for lunch the next day!

"Now what?" I started thinking, never having planned beyond what had just happened. And of course, I'd never been to the 21 Club, didn't even know where it was exactly. But everyone knew it was the place to eat and to be seen in New York, famous since Prohibition. So, the next afternoon, I wore my best dark blue suit and arrived half an hour before our scheduled meeting.

"I'd like your best table, please," I informed the maître d' in my most serious tone of voice.

"Certainly sir," he responded, then moved his hand out toward me.

I gripped it firmly, knowing that a strong handshake always made a good impression, but the expression on his face was far from what I expected. I didn't realize that the hand that shook the maître d's should have some cash in it to assist him in finding the best table for you.

I was promptly escorted to the table closest to the kitchen, with a view of the stove as waiters passed in and out of the swinging door. The table itself was barely large enough to hold the two glasses of water that had just been set down on top of it. And I sat, waiting through the longest minutes I'd ever endured in my life.

Finally, Mr. Hermann arrived. He was smaller than I'd imagined, quite short actually, but dressed very well and somewhere near seventy years old. He stood beside the table and shook my hand before sitting down, looking as though he were about to burst into laughter at any moment. Later he would confess that he guessed my age to be eighteen or less, and knew something was up the moment he set eyes on me. Of course, the table next to the kitchen was an additional clue as to my lack of stature. But at the time, I was convinced I was fooling him, and proceeded with my charade.

"So what was this deal you wanted to discuss young man?" he asked as they took our drink orders and presented each of us with a menu.

I started making up this huge lie, inventing most of it on the spot, "Well, the name I use is

Stanley Paul, but that's not my real name. My father's quite well known on Wall Street and I want to pursue a career on my own, without the family's influence."

"I see," he responded, looking intrigued. "And what career might that be exactly?"

I was starting to choke then, having opened the menu and glanced down the column of prices. This place was three times as expensive as any restaurant in West Chester. I began to worry that my first job in New York would be as a dish washer.

I closed the menu, hoping never to have to open it again, and continued my story. "I play the piano . . . very well, actually. I wouldn't waste your time if I wasn't good. But my parents are set against my getting involved with show business, and they certainly don't want their name dragged into it. Frankly, I don't want to capitalize on the family name either. If I told you their name, you would know it in an instant."

I kept repeating myself like this, talking a thousand words a minute. After only a few minutes, I'd no idea *what* I was saying! My mind was blank even though I continued speaking, filling up silence with a torrent of words.

Then, as luck would have it, our drinks arrived. I welcomed the interruption, using the moment to take out a handkerchief and wipe the sweat which had begun dripping on my suit, then sipped my drink which was a martini, with a twist. My instant response was to begin choking on my first truly dry restaurant martini. I only ordered a martini because that's what people drank in the movies, but I really didn't drink and had no conception of what I'd set myself up for. It began to dawn on me that perhaps I was not impressing this agent with my sophistication.

Mr. Hermann said nothing at all, not a word. "At least he is still sitting here." I thought,

"I must be doing something right." I never looked at the menu again, afraid I'd have a heart attack if I faced those prices. I ordered the Chicken Hash because I'd heard that was Joe DiMaggio's favorite. Maybe that would impress Mr. Hermann and, of all the things I might have ordered, it sounded the least expensive. I was wrong.

By the time we finished our lunches I'd calmed down considerably and we'd managed to have a very interesting discussion about music and musicians, what I wanted from life and what I might be able to do for him. If I was as talented as I said I was, he promised, he'd find me a job.

I couldn't believe what I was hearing! This was working out better than I could ever have imagined! Then the check came. My God! How could food and a couple drinks cost more than half a month's rent? Not to mention the tip, which I had no idea how to even calculate. I paid in a daze.

We went back to his office at Rockefeller Plaza together, where I sat down at the piano and started to play. I was sick and nervous, but the piano didn't know it. The songs seemed to almost play themselves. After I finished four or five of them, I relaxed enough to finally turn around to look at his face and he was grinning! I was so relieved I nearly passed out!

"You have a few rough edges . . . but I think you just might have what it takes." he said, holding out his hand for me to shake. Shaking was easy. By that time my whole body was shaking.

His last words to me were, "I'll see what I can do."

I stood as tall as I could as I headed for the door, trying to appear sure of myself. When the door closed behind me and I found myself in the hall facing the elevator, panic gripped me again. This was my only hope. Everything was riding on it.

I tried to be confident, but when three days passed and he still hadn't called, I began to worry. And each day after that brought more tension than I could handle. What if he didn't call at all? I couldn't very well call him again, could I? I didn't know what else to do. My only certainty was that I was not going to spend the rest of my life selling men's clothes in West Chester, Pennsylvania!

Then, an interminable week later, Mr. Hermann called and told me I'd gotten my first job. It was as though a death sentence had been lifted and I could feel myself breathing again as he explained where and when I was supposed to show up. He'd gotten me a trial run at a little place called the Piccolo Club on East 55th Street and Second Avenue, and I started the day after tomorrow!

I checked the place out the next day, and it was a far cry from the Versailles, or any of those chic clubs I'd heard so much about. But it was no corner piano bar either. It was a pretty good beginning, I decided, and I was determined to make a good impression.

To get the attention of the club owners, I drafted a few telegrams and sent them to myself on my opening night. "Sorry we couldn't make your opening." the first one said. "We know you'll be a smash!" Then I signed it, "Liz and Eddie." Remember, this was 1960 when Elizabeth Taylor and Eddie Fisher were America's most famous couple.

Another telegram was suppposed to come from Elsa Maxwell, "Wishing you only the best tonight and always. Your friend, Elsa". I'd read her name in the society columns, but I really had no idea who she was.

I waited for a reaction, but no one said a thing except Mr. Hermann, who thought it was odd that such famous stars were promoting the career of a kid whose parents didn't want their son to get involved in show business. and who was playing under an assumed name.

The only comment the owner made that night was to point out that I should spend my breaks mingling with the older female customers at the bar to make sure they kept drinking. I was to order whiskey, and the bartender would serve me iced tea. Was that really the reason my parents spent good money on all those piano lessons? To this day, I still have a hard time with tea, iced or otherwise.

When I wasn't on a break drinking iced tea with the grand dames, I was expected to accompany the chanteuse, Miss Adele, who looked like a refugee from Fredrick's of Hollywood. Whatever she wore showed off her great cleavage, which was a fortunate distraction from her lousy voice!

Just getting to and from the job each night was an unforgettable experience. One of the most glamorous clubs I'd ever seen, El Morocco, was just a few blocks away from the Piccolo on 54th Street. I always stopped there before showing up for work. El Morocco attracted the cafe society crowd who came to dance, mingle and be photographed as they alighted from Rolls Royces. The beautiful women who were dressed to the nines in furs, gorgeous gowns and fabulous jewels, would pass in an endless stream in and out of the club all night accompanied by men in black tie. I'd never seen anything even remotely like it before. I would just stand outside ogling everything and everyone until it was time to get myself to the more minuscule and far less grand Piccolo Club.

I finished work at four in the morning, and walked home along the deserted streets. I'd take the subway back to the Village, which in those days cost about fifteen cents. It was cheaper than a taxi, which I couldn't afford on my salary. It was not the danger zone subway stations are today. All sorts of weird characters could be seen shuffling in and out of cars, many of them probably head waiters or musicians, dressed in tuxedos just like me. I'd go home, change clothes, and often meet up with friends, then we'd all run to Chinatown to eat. New York really was the city that didn't sleep, always something open somewhere. By the time I was ready to call it a night, it was usually daylight and other people were just starting to get ready for work.

My trial run at the Piccolo was extended to a three-month engagement. Now that I finally had what I considered a job with some money coming in, I could really start exploring New York. The phrase "I'd died and gone to heaven" fit me perfectly. I spent every waking moment walking, listening, reading, practicing during the days and visiting the clubs in the hours before and after work.

Live entertainment was everywhere in New York in 1960. Every hotel had at least one dance band, the larger ones featuring headline entertainers. The Waldorf had Xavier Cugat, the Roosevelt featured Guy Lombardo, while Vincent Lopez and his orchestra were holding forth

Playing at the Piccolo Club.

at the Taft Hotel. The incomparable Hildegarde was still packing them in at the Persian Room of The Plaza. The ultimate in chic was the sultry Julie Wilson appearing in the Masonette Room at the St. Regis. The Latin Quarter, on the corner of Broadway and 48th Street, was owned by Barbara Walters' father. The Copacabana had stars like Frank Sinatra, Tony Bennett, and the Will Mastin Trio featuring Sammy Davis, Jr. I couldn't begin to afford the cover charges at these places, but once in a while I'd be able to stand at the door and get a glimpse of the performers.

And of course there was dancing! At the Palladium on Broadway you could dance all the new Latin crazes, like the Mambo and the Cha Cha. *Everyone* was learning them!

The east fifties, as the east side of town was called, were just filled with small night clubs featuring fabulous talent. Bobby Short, who was starting to make a name for himself, was at the Weylin Bar, and the wonderful Mabel Mercer was holding court at the RSVP on East 55th Street.

But it was the pianists that captured my attention in a way no other entertainer could. I'd spend hours listening to Cy Walter at the Drake Hotel and George Feyer at the Standhope, comparing myself constantly, admiring their skills and running home afterwards to practice.

I'd spend my afternoons rummaging through second hand stores and those wonderfully mysterious antique shops they had along Third Avenue in those years. My childhood preoccupation with collecting antiques had grown itself into a full fledged hobby by then and to this day remains a great source of personal enjoyment. I'd find old recordings, sheet music and all sorts of fascinating things people were foolish enough to be throwing away.

New York's Greenwich Village was a Mecca for unusual characters which gave the neighborhood its unique style. For instance, I'd hear Jackie "The Pay-Pah Lady" on the corner screaming "Pay-pah! Pay-Pah!!" in her thick British accent, with a sort of a Bronxish lilt to it. Jackie earned her nickname in the evenings when she hawked the papers she'd collected from the trash cans earlier that day. People claimed to have seen her going to the race track each day around noon, and that she was picked up and dropped off in a limo no less!!

At the time, I frequently ran into another unusual character, an odd looking girl who always caught my attention because she wore incredible get-ups combining red velvet skirts, gold 1920s style shoes, bizarre fabrics with clashing patterns and Cleopatra eye make up. She was always carrying shopping bags as she went in and out of the thrift shops that were also my favorites in my perpetual search for old music. Strange wasn't the word for her. She was outrageous and wonderfully weird. We never spoke. We never even met. But each time our paths would cross, she would be this memorable presence that set a new level of uniqueness.

I didn't have a very sophisticated repertoire, the scores of shows like *My Fair Lady, South Pacific* and *The King and I* were the only things I'd learned prior to coming to New York. So I'd listen to old phonograph records over and over again, trying to learn every new song from every musical. I'd digest anything by Cole Porter, Rogers and Hart or Gershwin, and I'd discovered new songs and new composers, like Cy Coleman and Kurt Weill. I realized that I had to learn gazillions of songs if I was going to keep up with the kind of talent that was playing the best clubs, and used every piece of 1920s and '30s sheet music I was able to get my hands on. When I was able to save a little money, my first major purchase was a second-hand piano. I was bringing home sheet music in shopping bags and learning to play virtually all of it. It seemed like I couldn't learn fast enough.

All my practicing paid off quicker than I might have thought when one night a very well dressed 'older' couple came into the club and sat at a table beside the piano. They were somewhere near fifty, which seemed old to me then, and had stopped in for a quick night cap on their way home from a night on the town. They seemed different somehow from the customers who'd regularly frequented the club, more sophisticated,. They ordered a drink and asked me to play *Miss Otis Regrets*, a song from the '30s.

I played it, by an odd coincidence having only just learned it, then played some other Cole Porter favorites, then a few by Noel Coward. They stayed for one drink after another and I managed to play just about every song from that era that I knew, grateful for those thrift shop searches and all that practicing I'd done.

They stayed until the club closed and asked what time I started the next night.

They were delighted when I answered, "Ten p. m." They asked if I'd care to play at an early party they were giving the next evening. I found myself agreeing without ever having discussed my fee. It wasn't till they'd left that I actually looked at their card and noticed the Park Avenue address. I'd walked past those great buildings hundreds of times by then, but I'd always wondered just who it was that lived there and what the view was like from inside. And now I was about to find out.

I put on my tux and showed up at their building at seven o'clock. As the doorman announced me I just stood there gaping. The foyer was huge, made of great marble squares that had been set down in a black and white checkerboard pattern. When I entered their living room I couldn't believe what I was seeing. It was as big as a restaurant, and decorated with antique furniture like nothing I'd ever seen! The wallpaper looked like it had been hand painted, and the draperies were made of some fabric I couldn't even begin to describe, great ornate hangings trimmed with thick fringes and oversized tassels that framed every window. A uniformed staff offered hors d'oeuvres and champagne to some thirty or forty guests. It looked like a scene from a Fred Astaire movie.

I took my place at the Steinway baby grand piano before a fifteen foot high window. No one was really paying any attention to me as I played, but I didn't care. It was like living in my fantasy and I was just pleased to be part of it.

Two hours later as I was leaving they handed me an envelope with fifty dollars in it. And they asked if I would be free the following Saturday for a "return engagement"? Would I! Fifty dollars for just a few hours work? I was making $125 a week at the Piccolo Club for six hours a night, six nights a week and drinking gallons of tea too!

"Certainly!" I said. I felt so rich I even splurged for a taxi home that night.

The next day I had business cards printed up with my name and phone number on them, then I set them on the corner of the piano at their party that next Saturday. People picked one up now and then, smiling and often slipping it into a pocket or pocketbook. Within a short time I was receiving quite a few calls to play for similar sorts of parties. I was on the 'playing for rich people' circuit, and loving it.

A few weeks later at one of these parties a very striking, older woman stood by the piano watching me for awhile, then asked "Could you play a little Cole?" I remember just gawking at her thinking "Who is this person? I think I've seen her picture in the paper or somewhere." I knew she had to be someone special since people seemed to be fawning all over her. I thought she might have been a silent film star or something.

She was quite regal, though not what I'd consider pretty and dressed so elegantly! When she

The Duchess of "Winza."

moved across the room, she just sort of floated. And the jewels she wore! I was mesmerized!

During my break I went into the kitchen, where I always went between sessions, and asked one of the kitchen helpers who "that lady standing by the piano" was.

"That's the duchess o' Winza!" I was told.

"Winza? Where's Winza?" I asked, never having heard of the place before.

"Not Winza, *Winza*!" she repeated, a sarcastic expression on her sour face. "Ya know . . . in England? The royal family? Ever hear o' *them*?"

"She's royalty?"

"No, of course not! You just don't get it, do ya?" her last words before she disappeared through the door with a tray of just filled champagne glasses.

"So who *is* she?" I asked the cook, still not the slightest bit enlightened.

"Ever hear of Wallis Simpson?" he said.

"You mean the woman who married the King of England?" I gasped.

"Well, thanks to her he ain't now!" he scowled, as voices from everywhere suddenly started in.

"Now, don't be sayin' such things! It's romantic what he done!" said the young girl with an English accent who was slicing lemons on the edge of the counter.

"Yaah, great." the cook answered them. "Some conquering hero he is now! Gettin' paid to show up at parties so's she can impress her friends! Meek as a mouse now, if ya ask me!"

"Well nobody asked you!" another young female voice chimed in. "And furthermore . . ."

Within minutes half the kitchen staff was in an uproar, arguing back and forth about whether or not he should have given up the throne to marry an ordinary woman and a divorced one at that! Not bad enough she was an American!

"Leave it to the kitchen help to fill you in!" I thought to myself as I quietly slipped back out into the living room, and remained behind my piano for the rest of the evening.

Then, just when I had almost more work than I could handle, my mother's health took a serious turn for the worse. I'd run to Pennsylvania Station every other day after about three hours sleep, in order to take the train to Philadelphia to see her there in the hospital. There wasn't time for more than an hour's visit before I had to hurry back to the station to catch the next train to New York to make it back in time for work.

Over those next few weeks she wasted away to no more than sixty pounds and finally, late in the summer, my sister called, urging me to hurry. I arrived by train early that morning, and our mother died in our arms later that same afternoon. Those days were sad and painful but I buried the pain deep inside somewhere. A sadness haunted my nights, sneaking into dreams and even quiet moments.

I had to leave my mother's funeral all too quickly. I had been gone three nights at that time and I got back just in time to keep from being replaced at the Club. It would be years before I'd finally have the time to mourn her properly. If I have a regret in my life that, without question, is it.

CHAPTER THREE

SMALL STEPS

Nights at the Piccolo were as they'd always been, and I wore a smile I put on along with my tuxedo for each evening's performance. But change was in the air and nothing in my life would ever be the same. I went running after my future one small step at a time.

The first step came in the form of an offer from William Rosen, who owned Gatsby's, an elegant and popular restaurant on First Avenue and 49th Street. He'd heard me play at a party one evening and offered me a job for $150 a week. Not only was it $25 more than I was already making, but it meant that my nights of sitting at the bar between sets pushing drinks were over. Along with the end to swilling iced tea, moving to Gatsby's meant I would no longer be accompanying the *incredible* voice of Miss Adele. I couldn't have been happier and accepted immediately! Even the atmosphere of the place was exhilarating, with ornately carved mahogany, red flocked wallpaper, Tiffany glass sconces and always a waiting line of well-dressed people for tables. But the best part of the whole thing for me was that sometimes the patrons would stop talking long enough to actually listen to me play!

I was seated at the piano one evening when this big buxom woman appeared with what seemed like the offspring of every chinchilla that

had ever mated draped over her ample shoulders. I guessed to be in her seventies. Sophie Tucker, the last of the "Red Hot Mamas," and her entourage slowly made their way to the table just in front of the piano.

Don't you think I look like Eddie Munster meets Tony Curtis?

"Hi ya, Soph!" one customer remarked after the other, but I'd recognized her before the first words were ever uttered, from appearances I'd seen on *The Ed Sullivan Show*. "If my father were only alive to see this!" I kept telling myself, my eyes glued to her table for the rest of the night.

She ate her dinner and, every few minutes, looked up at me approvingly as I played. Eventually, she came up to the piano and said, "You play some mighty fine piano kid."

After a few minutes of conversation, she said "Kid, I'm gonna give ya some advice. Anybody who says they like the way ya play, get their name and address, or their business card, and put them down in a book. Then, as you move from job to job, mail cards to everybody telling 'em where you'll be appearing and when. Buildin' up a following, they call it." She spoke with a serious expression on an otherwise jovial face, "That's the first step! Gotta have it! Don't you ever forget it."

Sophie Tucker gave me some valuable advice.

I listened carefully and thanked her for the advice. A little later, just as she was turning to leave, I blurted, "Miss Tucker?"

"Yes?" she responded.

"Do you happen to have a card . . . by the way?" I asked.

"Ahh, hah hah! The kid learns pretty quick!" she laughed as she handed it to me. "You know, my piano player Teddy was about your age when he started playing for me. Ya bring back a lotta memories!"

Within a few months, if anybody so much as said "hello" to me, I soon had their name and address. In those years postage was so cheap you could send out 50 cards for a buck and, little by little, I built up a following just as she'd said.

Later that fall I was able to sublet my own rent-controlled, large apartment on Grove Street in a much livelier section of the village. That was when $100 a month could get me a dream place of my own in New York. It took most of a weekend to move, although my "luggage" consisted mainly of dozens of shopping bags filled with sheet music.

A few days later, I decided to check out the neighborhood and found myself on Bleeker Street in Greenwich Village, following my nose into Zito's bakery and into the middle of a heated discussion.

"An angel I'm telling you!" a short, fat woman kept repeating. "So help me God, ya gotta hear it to believe it!"

"It's true!" the old man standing in front of Mr. Zito's counter confirmed. "I heard her before! Just the most beautiful thing you ever heard! Her voice I mean! Her *voice!*"

"She's a different one, I'll give ya that. That outfit she wore! Ahh . . . but you're right, that voice!" Mr. Zito said.

"Who's voice?" I asked.

"The singer at that club over on Eighth Street!" everyone seemed to say at the same time.

"Which club?" I asked, and I was promptly informed that it was called the Bon Soir.

Any voice that could get more attention than the delicious Italian bread at Zito's aroused my curiosity. I made a point of seeing her that very night. A young singer was the opening act for Phyllis Diller, who was just hitting the big time herself. The singer was very young, really just a girl, and not standard-issue attractive but she was everything the people in the bakery claimed she was and more! The first song she sang was *Keepin' Out of Mischief*, an old Fats Waller tune from the twenties, and when that voice sang I, like everyone else, was completely captivated.

But not only that, I recognized her! This was the unusual creature I'd been seeing on the streets around the thrift shops! The girl with all those shopping bags and the Cleopatra make up! And her name? If you haven't already guessed it was *Barbra Streisand!*

The job at Gatsby's was going great and my repertoire was growing. I even got my first mention in The New Yorker only six months into my professional career! Then, just a few weeks before

SEPTEMBER 3, 1960

GOINGS ON ABOUT TOWN

..... GATSBY'S, 873 First Ave., at 49th St., (PL 5-3775): A house divided by the piano of Stanley Paul, a newcomer to our *boîtes de nuit*, which stands between bar and dining room. He is on from eight to two, and his setting is satisfactorily ornamental. Closed Sundays and Labor Day. ...

(*New Yorker*, Sept. 3, 1960. Reprinted by permission)

Christmas, Henry Hermann asked me, "How'd you like to have your own trio?"

My voice betrayed my excitement, "Are you serious?"

"There's a catch though." He explained that I would have to leave the security of Gatsby's for a three-month engagement in Jamaica.

The position I had at Gatsby's was one any piano player would have given his eye teeth for, and I was scared to leave it. But I really wanted to be more than a piano player in a restaurant, no matter how high class the restaurant was. This was an opportunity to have my own group. I kept thinking, "A trio just like Bobby Short!"

I was booked at the Sunset Lodge in Montego Bay for an engagement that started on New Year's Eve and ran till Spring, and included room, board and a few hundred bucks a week, not to mention round trip airfare! I'd never even been on an airplane before, let alone out of the country for that matter!

I hired two Jamaican musicians, a bass player and drummer, who were so excited to be playing with an American musician that they always showed up for work two hours early. They didn't realize I knew less about what I was doing than they did, but I was catching on quickly. Everything was exotic, even the mostly older, British clientele who seemed straight out of *High Society* magazine. If this wasn't chic nothing was!

One evening, Noel Coward walked in! I couldn't believe it! The great Noel Coward! He had a house on the island and often stopped in for dinner, my musicians explained while I watched him being escorted to a nearby table.

"What an incredible co-incidence!" I thought to myself, having just learned a song that he'd written in the 1920s called *A Room with a View*. I decided to impress him by playing it but when I got to the middle section my mind went completely blank! I stumbled around a little, then changed to something else, hoping no one noticed. I was too embarrassed to even look up! I think even my elbows were sweating!

Instead of mingling with the guests as I usually did when the break finally came, I slipped out the back. I just stood around in the kitchen, pacing back and forth, calling myself every derogatory name I could think of and hoping he'd be gone by the time I came back. And he was, to my great relief.

I never felt so stupid in my life, and I practiced that song so much over the next few days I could play it in my sleep. A few weeks later he returned for dinner with a group of friends allowing me to launch into the song again, this time with no mistakes. Later as I walked past his table, I heard a distinctive, sophisticated voice say "Young man . . ." I stopped, turned, and faced him, completely frozen; motionless. He raised his glass, smiled and said, "I see you've been practicing."

I almost died! It was, however, another lesson in professional musicianship. I'd go out of my way from that point forward to research songs with some significance to visiting personalities and play a special tune for them whenever the opportunity presented itself, though only once I'd learned them, of course!

I stayed in Jamaica till April, and then came back to New York having missed winter. I wanted to put together another trio, but Mr. Hermann explained that there were no bookings available for me in the city with or without a trio. "I do have a part-time gig though, if you want it. Three nights a week, Thursday through Saturday, to the end of the summer. Interested?"

It was in a restaurant called Emily Shaw's, in Pound Ridge, New York, which was fairly close to the city, just an hour or so away. I could commute by train, or sometimes, if it was too late,

sleep overnight in a room at the top of the restaurant. "Better than selling suits . . ." I kept reminding myself.

I was there for just a few weekends when a couple I'd seen a few times finally introduced themselves. They were good customers at the restaurant and had often stayed for hours listening to me. The husband called me over to their table one night, and identified himself as Dr. William Nuland. He said, "You got a lotta talent, son. You're going be a big hit someday! Real big! You could use the advice of somebody like me. I've got a lot of connections in show business, believe me!"

"Call me Stanley." I said, shaking both of their hands, and wondering just how much they'd already had to drink. I was flattered but didn't really take him seriously. After a few drinks, a lot of people thought they were booking agents.

The following week they came back to hear me again and Dr. Nuland said,

"I'd like to manage you someday Stanley, think you might be interested?"

"Sure, someday. That'd be great!" I responded, but I was really just trying to be polite. I was barely making a living, let alone able to find the money to hire a manager!

"I know the perfect agent for you, too," he continued. "Name's Joe Glaser. Ever hear of him?"

Joe Glaser! I thought. Of course I'd heard of him! He headed up one of the biggest talent agencies in the United States. That a doctor from Bronxville knew somebody like that wasn't too likely. And even if he did, Joe Glaser handled only major stars. It would be a while before he'd be interested in me.

All summer long the Nulands continued to bring different people to hear me. When I'd look their way from the piano, they'd be nodding and smiling, raising a glass to offer a toast. I guessed they were having a pretty good time.

The summer gig at Emily Shaw's came to an end in the fall of 1961, and Henry Hermann was able to get me a full-time job. It was at a new restaurant called the Ponsette Room in the Wellington Hotel on Seventh Avenue and 55th Street. They didn't need a trio, just myself and a bass player named Lou Franco, but at least I was back in the city.

---

stanley paul

HIS PIANO IN EXCITING RHYTHMS

APPEARING NIGHTLY

PONSETTE ROOM	55TH & 7TH AVENUE
WELLINGTON HOTEL	NEW YORK CITY

Then six months later in March of 1962 my career moved to an entirely new plane. While I was still working at The Ponsette Room, Dr. Nuland called and told me he actually had set up an appointment with Joe Glaser himself! I couldn't believe it! All this time I thought he was only a doctor with more show business connections in his mind than in reality.

A few days later I walked into the building on the corner of Park Avenue and 57th Street and met Dr. Nuland in the waiting room of Associated Booking Corporation office. In a few minutes we were ushered in to meet the famous Joe Glaser in his big office. He greeted us with loudest voice this side of a cruise boat's horn!

"I hear you play the piano pretty good!" he announced, then grabbed the ringing phone.

"God damn it, I told you . . . THEY DON'T GET LOUIS ARMSTRONG! He's booked for Europe!" he screamed. Then he rocketed the phone into its cradle and turned to me.

"So where have you been playing? Do you play jazz? *Christ*, **you are** *young*, **aren't you?"** the voice boomed. Then back to the phone, **"Oscar, God damn it, tell 'em they've only got Dinah for two weeks . . . period. After that she's booked in Vegas."** he shouted, hung up, then picked up as if there had been no interruption.

"Kid, I don't know what we can do for you. Does Noel Kramer have your photographs and bio? I'm busy now. Good to meet you, kid." and we were done. I hadn't said a word.

We were lead out of his office and I just stood there, while Dr. Nuland was chattering with other Associated Booking Corporation agents. I was completely out of it, not knowing what to think. In those days, a musical agency like Associated Booking was almost like a major Hollywood studio. They had a lot of power, and were able to swing deals and make things happen pretty quickly.

When we left, I had no idea whether something would come of all this or not. But what an experience! Louis Armstrong! And that had to be Dinah Washington he was talking about! Definitely the big leagues. But how had Dr. Nuland been able to arrange that appointment with Joe Glaser himself? It was incredible.

Until that moment I hadn't understood the marvelous intriguing mind of Dr. Nuland. The doctor and his wife had been bringing a variety of key people into the Wellington to hear me, never telling me they were from Associated Booking Corporation. He'd casually introduce them as though they were friends of his, just ordinary people that happened to be with him on that night. Dr. Nuland was thinking I'd freeze up if I knew who they really were, and he was probably right. First he'd brought Noel Kramer, who was one of the agents. Then Oscar Cohen, who reported directly to Joe Glaser, was introduced as another

Dr. Nuland "friend." I have always been grateful for Dr. Nuland's behind-the-scenes strategizing.

A few weeks later I was told by Associated Booking that I'd be opening at Basin Street East. It was one of the hottest nightclubs in the city, and I'd be sharing the bill with the McGuire Sisters, who were at the height of their fame. I was to be the filler act, and as guests were being seated and ordering their drinks, I'd be playing as part of a trio. Filler or not, it was the biggest step my career had taken to date. Great exposure and working in such a famous place! I was on my way!

†**BASIN STREET EAST—137 E 48. PL 2-4444.** Jazz club featuring top-notch entertainment. The McGuire Sisters, Stanley Paul Trio at 9 & 12 (ex Sun) Fri. Sat. 8:30, 11:30 & 1:30. Dancing, Sun only, 2-7. No ent. Open 6 pm for cocktails. Chinese-Amer cuisine. D 7-3 a la carte from $3.75. Music charge in dining room $3. Fri. Sat. $3.50. Lounge $3. Sat min 2 drinks per person in bar. **CB, DC**

CHAPTER FOUR

UPS AND DOWNS

Suddenly everything was moving so quickly! I gave my notice at the Ponsette Room and Dr. Nuland drew up a contract for me to sign with him as my manager and Associated Booking as my new agency. Things were happening just as Dr. Nuland had predicted, but I still had a hard time believing it!

I was sent to Bruno of Hollywood to have a set of professional photos taken. It was in the Carnegie Hall Building on West 57th Street and I remember thinking how *classy* everything was suddenly getting. It was as though I were living in a dream, except that when I woke up I was still in it—practicing.

On opening night at Basin Street East, Dr. Nuland was there with a huge table of people, and my sister and her friends were at another just as big. I'd sent out notices to every single person on my mailing list, and a lot of them showed up. "At least I won't be booed off the stage." I thought. But I wasn't kidding myself. Most of the customers had come to see the McGuire Sisters and could have cared less about some piano player. The audience was polite, though, and while I didn't set the place on fire, I got pretty good reviews.

SHOW-BUSINESS
Saturday, April 7, 1962

Go East Young Man
To Basin Street East, that is, where Stanley Paul, the piano prodigy, is showing his versatility with his Trio nightly.

Stanley Paul, protege of Dr. Wm. Nuland, has broken into the New York scene with a bang—pianissimo now, but more forte every day as the night-club patrons catch his beautiful performance.

Suddenly everything was getting pretty fancy.

**NEW YORK
JOURNAL-AMERICAN
Tuesday, April 3, 1962**

Stanley Paul and his trio opened the show at Basin Street East. This young man is a very fine jazz pianist. Some night, some night club owner is going to stop a minute, listen to Stanley and blurt out: "Say, that young fellow can play piano!"

I'm saying that today—in print.

A few nights later, the management told me that they were going to hold us over for the next headliner who would be Miss Peggy Lee! The year before she'd had a huge hit with a live recording called *Peggy Lee at Basin Street East.* But then she came down with an illness, and dropped out of sight. Rumors were that it was emphysema and that her condition was very serious. Opening night was her first public performance since she'd become ill, and the place was packed. Everyone who was *anyone* had come to see her, and even people who weren't!

I walked out onto the stage and started playing, looking around the room now and then to see if I recognized anyone. Seated right in front of me was the legendary composer Richard Rodgers with his daughter, Mary. I was nervous from that point on. I finished my 20-minute set to polite applause, but everyone was just glaring at me, as though doing so would make Peggy Lee appear that much sooner. I couldn't wait to get off!

When I got backstage, all was chaos! Pandemonium! People were running all over as though the place had just caught fire. "Get some oxygen in here!" someone screamed, and almost immediately two guys carrying a tank plowed their way through the onlookers. I just stood there with my mouth hanging open till someone came up and started shaking me.

"What the hell's the matter with you!" he was screaming at me. "Get back out there and play for God's sake!"

"I can't go back out there." I started to explain, then felt myself being thrown onto the stage.

"She won't be ready for at least twenty minutes." someone shouted. "Just *play* something!"

I could hear a groaning sigh from the audience the moment I re-appeared on the stage. "What's *he* doing back?" someone said, offering probably the most tepid welcome of my life. I tried to pretend I didn't hear and started into some Gershwin. The crowd paid absolutely no attention to me, murmuring and sighing louder and louder. This continued for twenty long minutes. Just as I imagined that a lynch mob was forming, she was finally ready!

"And now . . . Miss Peggy Lee!" the announcer shouted, and the house erupted in cheers. I'd never heard such a roar and scrambled off the stage to get out of her way.

**NEW YORK
JOURNAL-AMERICAN
Tuesday, April 17, 1962**

The show was opened by pianist Stanley Paul and his trio. I've written it before and I'll write it again—Stanley Paul is more than a promising newcomer. He's a young musical star who is here right now.

After her complete recovery there were no more emergencies or delays and for the next two weeks each performance was pure magic, Peggy Lee was so nice! She'd call me by name as I walked past her dressing room. She was that way with everybody! (As opposed to the McGuire Sisters who'd never so much as looked my way, let alone actually spoken to me!)

A few days later Dr. Nuland announced, "Decca Records is going to sign you to a contract." I was to record the title song from a movie about to be released called *My Geisha,* starring Shirley MacLaine and Yves Montand. "A *movie!*" I kept repeating excitedly.

I was given the music, informed that the recording date was the next week, and sent to Steinway

Peggy Lee was a doll to me.

Hall on West 57th Street to pick out the piano I'd play for the recording session. "Pick a piano from a selection of *Steinways*?" I whispered to myself, "and only a few months ago I was lucky to have something to play that was in tune!" I chose one from among a dozen fabulous instruments, and was told that Van Cliburn had just used that same piano for his last recording. Although I still suspected that I must be dreaming, I couldn't help but think, "Pretty decent company."

I practiced the song till I could play it backwards and forwards. When I entered the studio, I was totally prepared. Henry Jerome, a well known band leader with Decca Records, was there to conduct what looked like an entire symphony orchestra. The chorus was the size of an opera choir. Dick Jacobs, also with Decca, had written the very lush orchestral arrangement of the *My Geisha* that I'd practiced. I was petrified, but got through the session with no retakes.

We recorded the flip side *When I Fall In Love* pretty quickly, and I was on my way home again in about two hours. I'd expected it to take all day, but they paid by the hour and couldn't afford to spend time dealing with mistakes. I was told my first record was to be released under the Coral Records label, that I'd done well, and that they had *big plans* for me. "We'll make you into another Roger Williams or Carmen Cavellero," they said, and as far as I was concerned, they could just make me into anyone they wanted.

The Basin Street East gig ended, and my trio was booked at the Mermaid Room of the Park Sheraton Hotel, at Seventh Avenue and 55th Street. It was just across the street from the Wellington, where I'd played only weeks before. On opening night I almost *wrecked* the joint!

The room was decorated in some sort of under water theme, with naked mermaid forms hanging from the ceiling. Someone had draped them in fish netting, so as not to offend some of the patrons, I suppose. The piano was on a big platform in the center of this huge circular bar, controlled by a switch that the bartender operated to make it rotate, with three of the mermaid forms hanging just above it. I decided to open the top of the piano, in order to make the whole spectacle a little more dramatic, and as I started to play the stage began to rotate. But unbeknownst to the management, the open piano top caught one of the mermaid's fishnet outfits as it turned around. Soon I heard this deep, rumbling sound as the entire ceiling decoration started falling apart! Creaking sounds were starting to come from the ceiling.

Everyone in the audience was staring at me and pointing, as I made strange gestures and hysterical facial expressions trying to get the bartender's attention. Finally, just as I was about to have a heart attack, one of the waiters realized what was going on and frantically signaled the bartender to turn off the rotating stage. I continued to play one song after another throughout the crisis, and the audience roared in appreciation for such an unexpectedly entertaining show! From then on I played with the top of the piano in its closed position after being informed by the management that I should not come up with any more new ideas.

Unlike the mermaids, I got a lot of exposure. Performances from the Mermaid Room were broadcast on radio live three nights a week, for the New York, New Jersey and Connecticut listening audiences. I'd get calls from friends and extended family members, telling me they'd heard me. Some of them I hadn't seen since childhood! It was amazing!

The Mermaid Room gig continued for several months. Meanwhile, the *My Geisha* record finally came out, and I was sent to every radio station within hearing distance to visit the disc jockeys and give them free copies so they'd play it. Decca set up a promotion schedule for me, and there were notices in *Variety*, *Billboard* and *Cashbox* saying wonderful things about the record. Even Dr. Nuland was flying around all over the country promoting it!

The movie was finally ready to open at the DeMille Theater on Broadway, and I was instructed by Decca Records to distribute the 45 records to the first hundred people who showed up. I had to almost force people to take the records though. The people who came to see the movie couldn't have cared *less* about the record! They never heard of Stanley Paul, and the title song didn't mean anything to them either.

My Geisha couldn't hold a candle to the popularity of the scandalous film *Lolita*, with Sue Lyon and James Mason, that was opening at the Loews Theater down the street that same night. It was the talk of the town, all I'd been reading about in the papers for days, and a big Hollywood type premiere was scheduled just a few hours later that evening. Disappointed by the reception I'd had at the *My Geisha* opening, I concocted a new plan.

"I have a wild idea!" I told Dr. Nuland.

Little did they realize they were going to get me as part of the bargain!

"Stanley, you always have a wild idea!" was all he said, but he was listening.

"Could you call a few talent agencies and see if you can hire us a geisha?" I grinned back at him. "She doesn't have to be authentic, just someone who can play the role."

"Why? What are you planning to do?" he asked, instantly suspicious.

I replied, "Don't worry about it. Just trust me. And, by the way, how much would it cost to rent a Rolls Royce?"

Next I called his teenaged daughter, and asked her to bring all her girlfriends to the theater. "Forget it!" she said, but changed her mind when I offered a dollar apiece for each of them to mob me when I got out of the Rolls at the *Lolita* opening.

I ran back to my apartment, grabbed my oldest of the three tuxedos I'd now acquired, then paid a visit to my friend Bella, the Hungarian tailor. I asked her to take the suit apart and baste it together again so that it could be easily ripped apart.

"But vhy?"

"Please do it! Will you?" I screamed at her. "Can it be ready in a few hours? I really need it!"

"Vhat's going on? You do some trick in show?" she said, her eyes wide open and glaring at me.

"*At* one!" was all I said. "But we've only got a few hours! *Please* hurry!"

I ran down the block to the local art store, bought paint, brushes and some cardboard, and started putting together placards announcing "STANLEY PAUL FAN CLUB!" or "STANLEY IS OUR IDOL!"

I ran back to Bella's, who handed over the tux and charged me $20. "Goot luck!" she yelled after me as I went scrambling back through the door.

Dr. Nuland's daughter and twenty of her friends came to pick up their signs thirty minutes ahead of schedule. Then Dr. Nuland called to say he'd spoken with his friend, Art Ford, the disc jockey. By a stroke of good fortune Art was hired to announce the arrivals of the celebrities at the *Lolita* premiere. He promised to make a big fuss when I showed up.

Everything was set. I was walking around the apartment in my tux like Frankenstein, unable to sit for fear of coming apart at the seams. The Rolls Royce, which cost fifty dollars, arrived with Dr. Nuland inside of it. The geisha was waiting curbside in full costume. On the way to the theater, I tried to explain every detail of my plan to her. She merely smiled sweetly and bowed her head. I never realized she was the real thing until Dr. Nuland informed me she spoke no English.

At 46th and Broadway, I stuck my head out of the car to get an idea of the size of the crowd. Not enough people had showed up, so we turned around, killed about twenty minutes, then came back for another pass. By that time, the place was mobbed!

The Rolls pulled right up in front of a red carpet that had been laid out for the movie stars' arrival. As we slowed to a stop, I heard Art Ford's voice booming over the microphone "He's *HERE*! The teenage idol, Stanley *Paul*! With his new hit record, *My Geisha*!"

Seconds before my clothes were ripped to shreds by my paid fans.

"Teenage idol?" The last time I was a teenager I was still living at home with my parents in West Chester, Pennsylvania.

As I got out of the car, all my paid fans began screaming. They were waving their painted signs, crying, yelling and mobbing me as I tried to make my way to the microphone. When I started throwing out records, the girls jumped on me and began tearing my tux to shreds! The news photographers were going wild by now, bulbs flashing everywhere, fans screaming in a chaotic frenzy. It was perfect! Pandemonium according to plan! Except the poor geisha girl had no idea as to what to expect. She bolted back to the car and stood there, absolutely frozen! Her beautiful almond eyes had grown to the size of Brazil nuts as Dr. Nuland stood beside her, trying to calm her down.

Someone from Seven Arts, who'd legitimately promoted the *Lolita* event, kept asking "What the hell is going on? Who *is* this guy?" But his words were drowned out by the crowd as someone shouted to the star of the film, Sue Lyon, "Go stand with Stanley Paul!" And she *did!*

"Who's Stanley Paul?" someone said from what sounded like the far edge of the crowd. "I don't know!" someone answered him, "But everyone else sure seems to!"

Sue Lyon, James Mason and Shelley Winters made their way through the crowd and into the theater, and I was ushered in after them, then out a side door and back to the waiting car. I never even got to see the movie until years later on TV. We dropped the geisha off at the spot we'd picked her up, and I changed into my non-basted tuxedo in the car as we sped to the club. I started that evening's performance at the Mermaid Room only fifteen minutes late, completely out of breath and thanking God that I hadn't been fired.

The movie *My Geisha* hadn't exactly thrilled the critics, so after no more than a few weeks my record was hardly getting any air play. Decca did

say, however, that they were pleased with my performance and that they'd find something else for me to record very soon. Though the movie and the record hadn't done particularly well, my publicity stunt had excellent results. I was starting to get noticed and soon received an offer to be part of a program that was being sponsored by the Junior Achievement Society of New York and was going to be presented at *Carnegie Hall.*

"Carnegie Hall!" There was one place I'd never in my wildest dreams imagined myself appearing. Carnegie had probably been in my parents' fantasies for me back in the days when they'd been envisioning my future as a concert pianist.

Cab Calloway was on the bill, and for my bit I'd been asked to play several selections from *West Side Story.* I was very nervous, to say the least.

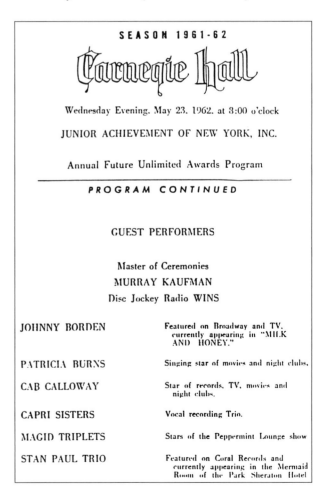

Carnegie Hall program.   (Used by permission)

In good company, Summer of 1962, but within 3 months, I was on the unemployment line!
Source: Daily News Wednesday, June 13, 1962

Because I was thoroughly familiar with the music, within a few minutes of sitting down at the piano on the stage, I relaxed and had the time of my life. The acoustics were like nothing I'd ever experienced, and the exhilaration of playing in such a magnificent place was simply indescribable. It was a night I'll never forget.

The Mermaid Room had turned out to be my most enjoyable gig to date. I was starting to get some local attention, but I was exhausted. Between the *My Geisha* promotions, daytime wanderings and working nearly every night, I hardly ever slept. I needed a vacation. My summer contract ended in the middle of August, so I took a vacation during the last two weeks of the month before starting the new season in September.

I went to the Pocono Mountains in Pennsylvania with some friends. Just drove around, slept late, went to bed early and relaxed for the first time in a long time. About five days into my vacation, I called Dr. Nuland and asked when I was expected back at the Mermaid Room.

"I hate to tell you this," he said, "but they didn't re-sign you for the fall season. They liked you but they wanted a change and got someone else."

Needless to say the vacation was ruined. I was ruined! And things were really beginning to change in New York in the fall of 1962 as far as the Club scene was concerned. Places that had featured live entertainment the year before were closing left and right. After a few weeks of *no prospects*

I found myself in the unemployment line, collecting fifty dollars a week and grateful for my rent controlled apartment.

Despite my jobless state, I still had recording contracts with Decca Records, but the songs they selected were real doozies. The next one they chose for me to record was *Phantom of the Opera*,

"Was I ever this young?"

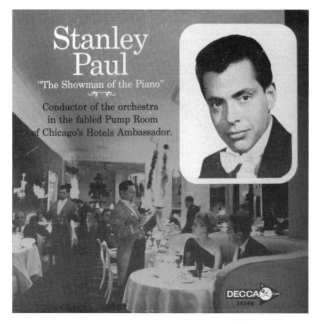

Recycling Stanley Paul.

the 1962 English movie version, not the one by Andrew Lloyd Webber. We recorded it at the same studio, same piano, same orchestra, same chorus. Decca even took out a full page add in Cash Box and Billboard to promote it. It was an absurd situation, really. I'm in the unemployment line, can't find a job and there's a full page add in Cash Box and Billboard with my smiling face plastered across it! Irving Berlin really knew what he was saying when he wrote *There's No Business Like Show Business!*

The Phantom of the Opera bombed, just like *My Geisha* had done before it. The people making decisions at Decca about what would succeed and what wouldn't were making some major errors in those days. They'd turned down a group from Liverpool only days before, a group that called themselves the *Beatles.*

It seemed Decca came to the conclusion that I wasn't going to be another Roger Williams after all, because they decided to produce an album featuring the Stanley Paul Trio. The setting was a candlelit nightclub with real live people in the audience, recorded late in the evening to make me feel more comfortable. The album was called *Cocktail Hour with the Stanley Paul Trio,* and though it never made the charts, sales were less than embarrassing. It would be re-released a few years later, while I was in Chicago playing at the Pump Room, under a new title, *Stanley Paul at the Pump Room.* I guess it was the record industry's version of recycling.

Finally, after being out of work for a few months, we were booked into a popular spot on Long Island called Andres of Great Neck early in 1963. I didn't own a car, and Long Island was a good distance away, so I took the subway to the Bronx, where my bass player lived, then drove the rest of the way there with him. Then, after the club closed each evening, we'd do the same trip in reverse and he'd drop me off back in the Bronx at the subway station. If I missed the 2 am train, as I often did, the next train wouldn't come along for what seemed like hours. I was stranded with no options but to sit at that deserted subway station and wait, hoping I wouldn't get mugged, and as the months went on I'd grown thoroughly sick of it. I wanted to get back to Manhattan!

But I'd learned my lesson well. I was never going to leave a job again until I had another prospect on the horizon, so I stayed there for almost ten months.

**STANLEY PAUL TRIO
OPENING NOV. 4th**
CRYSTAL ROOM
316 East 54th Street
N. Y. C.
Dining & Dancing
NIGHTLY 9 - 3 *
✦
Hope to see you
STANLEY

* EXCEPT SUNDAYS

Late in the fall we were booked into the Crystal Room on East 54th Street, a small club practically across the street from El Morocco. Our stay there was pretty uneventful, nothing much happening in November of 1963, except for one thing that made it *unforgettable* for me and most every other person in the country. Ask anyone who was alive then what they were doing that day and they'll probably remember what they were doing the day President Kennedy was shot.

I called the owner shortly after hearing the news, expecting that the club would probably be closed that night. Mrs. Storch, whose son Larry would later become the co-star of the popular TV comedy show *F Troop*, asked, "Why would we close? After all, he wasn't related to us!"

We were one of the few establishments of any kind that remained open that night and, except for the staff, the place was deserted.

In 1964 jobs were getting harder and harder to find as fewer clubs were featuring any live entertainment. A new word called *discotheque* had entered the vocabulary. Suddenly, all a club needed was a turntable and some loudspeakers.

But I was convinced there had to be a lot of people who still wanted to hear the kind of music I loved to play. I'd show up in my agent's office every afternoon looking for work, making a nuisance of myself from their point of view, I suppose. Then some friends from my days at Gatsby's heard I'd been looking for a gig and offered me a job at the Polonaise, a new restaurant they'd just opened on East 51st Street. It was just me and my bass player, and I *loved* that job, for one big reason—the tips were fantastic!

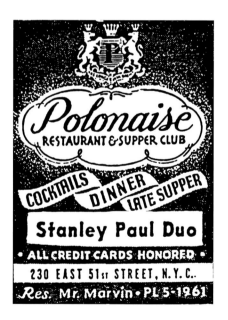

After the club closed each night around 2 am, they'd lock the doors and everyone still there would gather around my piano and sing. It was usually the same crowd night after night, so we got to know each other pretty well and had some great times. Everybody seemed to think they were professional singers after they'd had a few drinks, and as the enthusiasm rose so did the tips.

Nothing less than a ten dollar bill ever found its way to my piano. I'd learned most every saloon song that had ever been written by then and was taking home several hundred dollars a week in tips alone! In cash no less!

Meanwhile, Associated Booking had been trying to get me a booking at the Embers on East 54th Street. It was New York's premiere jazz club, home of such well known personalities as Dorothy Donegan and Erroll Garner. It was a real stepping stone. If you did well there, it was easy to get bookings in big name jazz places all over the country.

Associated Booking's efforts finally paid off, and they got me a trial run for a Sunday evening. If I went over with the audience, they said, I might be asked back . . . or not. It was up to me to win an engagement. No guarantees. The fact that I wasn't a jazz pianist was something I never focused on. I'd learned that I could hold my own wherever I played, so far at least, just by playing what customers wanted to hear.

That first Sunday the selections I chose seemed to go over pretty well. No jazz, but the audience seemed to really enjoy the music. As I was leaving that night, I was invited to return the following Sunday. I'd hoped for an offer of a few weeks at least, but wasn't about to complain. But when the telephone rang a few days later, I was more than surprised to hear Mr. Glaser himself on the line!

"Heard they asked ya back at the Embers next Sunday." he screamed in his usual tone of voice.

"Yes, that's right . . ." I began, starting to apologize for not having been offered a longer gig, but he didn't hear a word I said.

"Well Stanley, you got a month booking at the joint, you'll be opening on August 5th." he added, as I listened, speechless. **"Proud of ya kid, just called to tell ya. Keep it up!"** he shouted and, before I could get a word in, he was gone.

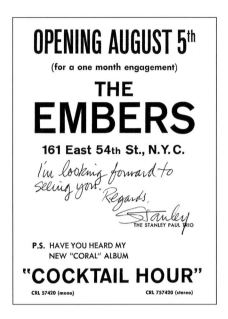

I couldn't believe my ears! This was the best club in New York! And a *jazz* club at that! And Mr. Glaser actually called me *himself!* I wasn't about to let him down or myself either, for that matter. I was gonna knock their socks off!

The next Sunday night went even better than the previous one. Everything seemed to click. The audience seemed to like us, lots of applause at the end of each set, people even started singing along to the songs. In a jazz club! The management didn't seem to mind either and when we left that night I was on cloud nine! But the next day, when I picked up the *Herald Tribune* I couldn't believe what I was reading. The jazz critic hated me, said I was "ruining the club" and didn't appreciate the "sing along atmosphere" I was creating. It was as if I'd organized an invasion of the hallowed ground of jazz. "And he never stops looking at his audience and smiling!" he wrote. He ended the review with "Solid applause at the end of his set . . . oh well."

I would learn later that Joe Glaser hadn't been too pleased about the negative reviews. During lunch with another client, Erroll Garner, the famous pianist, the subject of "what to do with Stanley Paul" came up.

"It's obvious he's no jazz pianist." Erroll Garner pointed out, then added "But you know he might make a decent society band leader, between that smile of his and those medleys he plays."

"You've got a point." Mr. Glaser agreed. "That's what a society band leader is—a smiling medley player!"

While Associated Booking was wondering what to do with me, some people had seen me playing at the Embers and thought that my smile would be "perfect" for the show they were doing. It was a musical variety show called *The Latin Touch* to be filmed in Lisbon, Portugal. I had to get a map out to figure out just where it was! I'd be recording a special arrangement of the big Broadway hit of that year, *Hello Dolly*. The famous Latin band leader Xavier Cugat was the emcee, a well-known personality, but the production was to be distributed in the Latin American market so it was unlikely anyone I knew would ever see it. (And as it turned out, I never have seen the show.) What made it so exciting was that I'd be paid $1000 plus airfare, a fortune for me, for a week of my time in Lisbon, then three days in Madrid for a follow-up filming.

I ran out and bought a copy of *Europe On Five Dollars A Day* . I wanted to spend as much time as I could exploring since airfare home was already paid for. I was paid up front and quickly converted the money to traveler's checks, then about two weeks later I was on my way. The *Hello Dolly* arrangement was complicated though, and I hadn't gotten it in my hands till a couple days before I left. All the way over on the plane I kept playing it over and over a thousand times in my head.

It was Sunday afternoon in Lisbon when the plane set down. "The Ritz!" I instructed the dri-

ver, and we were off. The city was so *clean*, and the boulevards were so *wide*, not the crowded congestion I'd gotten so used to at home in New York.

That night I had dinner with the film representative who'd discovered me at the Embers, then got to bed early to be sure to be prepared for filming the next day. But I didn't sleep at all. I was wide awake rehearsing the *Hello Dolly* number in my head all night. By morning I was exhausted. I showed up at the studio at 8 a.m., more nervous than when I'd gotten off the plane. The crew spoke no English, nor did most anyone else, except for the translator, my soon-to-be constant companion.

Performs With Xavier Cugat

Stanley Paul on European Tour

Pianist Stanley Paul has been selected to perform on two International Television Spectaculars originating in Europe. The first one was taped in Lisbon, Portugal on Monday and the second is to be taped tomorrow in Madrid, Spain. His co-stars are the renown band leader Xavier Cugat, and singers Katrina Valente and Dorothy Dandridge. Mr. Paul is backed by a 27-piece orchestra when he offers a surprise version of the new Broadway hit "Hello Dolly."

Some tour! I came back with 37 cents in my pocket.

The whole situation was getting increasingly uncomfortable. Again and again we played the arrangement. After the second try I managed to get through the number with no mistakes. "You're not smiling enough!" they criticized. It was why they'd hired me in the first place, they kept saying. They didn't seem pleased, and I just kept getting more and more nervous.

That night in bed was just like the one before. I didn't get a single minute's sleep. I just kept staring at the clock, watching it move from one five minute segment to the next, till finally morning came, and we started all over again.

Those days films were made in pieces, then edited together later. The previous day's films had to be interchanged with today's, so the movements of my hands over the keys had to be exactly the same! The arrangement included a lot of runs up and down the keyboard. Wherever I looked, men and women in the crew were holding their lips apart with both forefingers in grotesque grins as a signal to me to smile more. When I did smile, it seemed so phony that I was sure I looked like Alfred E. Newman, the icon of Mad Magazine.

I was a wreck by the time we finished, and went directly to my room to try to get some sleep. But, like every other night, exhausted as I was, sleep just would not come. Finally, I had an idea! I called room service and ordered "a double." "A double *what?*" they asked, to which I responded "Anything!" I wasn't a drinker, and couldn't really tell bourbon from scotch. All I can say for sure,

though, was that whatever arrived certainly wasn't iced tea, because half an hour later I was sound asleep.

The next day everything fell into place. Either because of sleep deprivation or incipient alcohol poisoning, I was relaxed, and finally enjoying myself. We finished our segment, with me smiling all the way through it, and three days later were on our way to film a television show in Madrid. Show business people weren't allowed at the Ritz in Spain in those days, so we had to stay at the Hilton.

When we finished up in Madrid I toured Europe with no bookings at all for three more weeks, staying in cheaper and cheaper hotels as what was left of my thousand dollars quickly vanished and I finally went home. A friend met me at the airport when I got back and took me home in her car. Thank God! I'd spent almost everything I had by then, and only had 37 cents left! But I was so much *older* now, it seemed to me. Wiser for all the experiences. And poorer. And looking for work again.

A NEW DIRECTION

The club situation that was scaling down in New York months before was even worse by the fall of 1964, so I played the first two weeks after my return at the Dune Deck, a club in the Hamptons. Before I had much time to worry about my next gig though, I was offered a return engagement at Andrés in Great Neck. Riding the subway was better than standing in the unemployment line, so I accepted and then lined up a bass player and drummer.

Not long after I'd gotten resettled at Andrés, Mr. Glaser showed up *himself* with two other men I'd seen there the week before. They sat through a set and then Mr. Glaser called me over to the table. He explained that they were looking for a band leader at the "Pump Room" because a band leader named David LeWinter, who had played there since the mid 1940s, had just left.

"It's in Chicago." Mr. Glaser was saying. "Heard of it? Ambassador East Hotel?"

I hadn't heard of the Pump Room. But *leading a band!* Except for those few recordings I'd made for Decca, I had no experience with a *band*! They wanted me to start in three weeks! "Would I be ready?" they were asking, while I sat there paralyzed.

"Of *course* he'll be ready!" Mr. Glaser glared at me, smiling. **"Won't you, son!"** he boomed.

"Sure," I agreed, then returned to the piano in absolute panic.

During my break I told my bass player and drummer what had just happened, along with the fact that I didn't know how to lead a band! "And I've never even heard of the place!" I added.

"Really? You never heard of the Pump Room?" both replied.

"No." I confessed again. "Why? Is it that well known?"

"Yaah . . . I'd say so." the drummer laughed. "Dinner, dancing, movie stars coming in all the time. And all the food is served on flaming swords, I hear."

Movie stars? And dancing? I wasn't laughing. "How am I gonna do this?"

"Don't panic, just do what you're doing now," they reassured me. "The only difference is you have to change the keys around so that they'll be in the right range for the horns."

The next day, I ran out and bought every Lester Lanin record I could find. I practiced non stop for the next three weeks, reworking every song I knew into keys that could accommodate all the instruments. And every night I checked out another club, listening to as many of the top bands in New York as I could.

Most of the songs they played were the ones I'd learned these past few years. The arrangements were similar, identical half the time, but the keys were different. Also, they never played more than one chorus of a song before moving to the next. The medleys had been redefined and polished so that one song flowed almost unnoticeably into another.

When my friends and some of the customers at Andrés asked where it was I'd be going, I was surprised again and again by how many people had heard of the Pump Room, its flaming swords, movie stars and celebrities. Someone even said the Queen of England had been there once.

Still I was apprehensive. It was a step up, certainly, to lead a band. Just as leading a trio in Jamaica had been a step up from *piano player*. But as great as Montego Bay had been, I was isolated, on a small island in the middle of nowhere. A stepping stone maybe, but not the place to build a career. And the trip to Europe had been pretty exciting, but nothing much seemed to come of that either. A big part of me believed that I should stay where I was and take my chances here in New York. All the action was *here*, wasn't it?

On the other hand, if things worked out well in Chicago, who could say where that job could lead? It was a new direction, and a real opportunity.

I made arrangements to have my mail forwarded, and when the departure date finally arrived, I packed a couple bags and caught a taxi to La Guardia. It was nearly nine o'clock and it was cold, dark and raining as I stepped into the cab at Chicago's O'Hare Airport. "The Ambassador East Hotel." I told the driver. "State and G . . . , Go . . ."

"State and 'Go-thhheee'," he finished for me, and twenty minutes later we were pulling up to the hotel.

"Welcome to the Ambassador East, sir," the doorman greeted me, motioning to the bellman.

I followed my luggage through the entrance and up the stairs toward the lobby, and the first thing I laid my eyes on was a giant poster framed in glass. It was displayed on a large wooden pillar in the center of the room, and my photograph was plastered across the top of the poster and beneath it the words:

Stanley Paul and
His East Coast Society Orchestra Opening in the Pump Room Wednesday Night

"Stanley Paul and his *what*?" I said the words out loud. I had no orchestra of my own at all, let alone an *East Coast Society* one!

"That's our new band leader, sir," the clerk behind the desk informed me. "Welcome to the Ambassador East! Have you stayed with us before?" she asked, smiling.

"Well no, actually . . ." I began, my eyes still glued to the poster, then I slowly turned to my right to face her and check in.

"Why you're *him!*" she said, and pointed in the direction of the Pump Room just down the hall as she handed me my key.

(Chicago Historical Society photo)

The famed Pump Room.

and within five minutes was hurrying back downstairs to check out this Pump Room of theirs! Finally!

I made a quick right turn from the elevator and climbed up the three thickly carpeted stairs, and then entered through the leftmost of the two great glass doors at the entrance, the one that led to the bar. The maitre d' stationed to the right was speaking with a customer, but gave me a quick glance and a nod. I took the closest of several available bar stools, ordered a ginger ale and looked back toward the entrance.

A podium stood between the two glass doors, with what looked like one of the thickest antique books I'd ever seen open on top of it. And mounted just above it, on the wall that separated

I could hear the music playing as I stood there in the lobby, and I could smell the food, but I couldn't see very far beyond its giant arched opening, the words PUMP ROOM spelled out just above it. There was a narrow column down its center, separating two etched glass doors that opened out to the lobby, and as I approached the elevator just a few feet from the entrance, I was tempted to poke my head through the doorway and take a quick look inside, but decided to wait. I'd go upstairs and change into something more appropriate first. I accompanied the bellman to my room, which was small but very tastefully decorated, tipped him, then ripped my suitcases open the moment he left. I changed into my navy blue Brooks Brothers suit,

Pump Room, another view.

(Chicago Historical Society photo)

the doors, was a large green and silver colored pump—the kind with a *handle!* The walls of the room were a lacquered navy blue and three gigantic crystal chandeliers were suspended over the center of the dining room, reflecting flames from some of the swords I'd heard so much about and bouncing the reflections all over the room.

But the costumes! The waiters were wearing red swallowtail cutaway coats and black shoes with large silver buckles. Some of them were carrying flaming swords, and some weren't. And the man pouring coffee! He was dressed in a long green jacket of a similar style and trimmed with thick white embroidery, and green knee britches with white stockings pulled up to the hems. He wore a white

(Chicago Historical Society photo)
Make way for swords with flaming food.

The costumes! The flames!

Two Eddies: Actor Eddie Albert with Eddie, the famed coffee server.

silk turban with huge white feathers sticking up from the top of it! He stood a few feet from the table he was serving, with the coffee pot in his hand, arm extended, pouring a long stream of steaming, dark brown liquid into the cup from far above it.

The waiters carried a few swords of flaming food, though not many were lit that night. The room was nearly empty as a matter of fact. Every now and then, a metal wagon came clamoring down an aisle bringing food to a waiting table.

"What's with the wagons?" I asked the bartender.

"Kitchen's in the basement," he explained. "They bring the food up in the elevator and keep it warm in the wagons. Bring it right through those doors." he said, pointing toward the far right corner of the room, just opposite the dance floor.

"Is that why they light all the food on fire? To keep it warm?" I laughed.

"Partly," he smiled. "Most of it's just the theatrics, that's what people remember. Pretty dramatic, don't you think?"

Dramatic was the word alright! The whole thing was like an 18th century play! Or an opera that became too grand.

"I expected to see celebrities. Where are they?" I asked.

"Well, let's see." he said, squinting. "Oh there! There's Carmel Meyers over there in that booth." he said pointing out a leather banquette near the center.

"*Who?*" I stared at him.

"Hey! She once made a movie with Rudolph Valentino. Ever hear of *him*?"

"Wonderful . . ." I thought to myself. Then I suggested, "Maybe Adolph Menjou will come join her!"

The bartender shot back, "He was here many times . . . before he died."

"Even better," I thought, but kept that to myself.

Way across the room, in the far left corner, a small orchestra was playing *Strangers in the Night* over and over and over. "Pretty appropriate," I thought as I looked at my watch. It was only 11:30 and most of the customers had fin-

ished and already gone home for the evening. The white leather booths that lined the room were as attractive as I'd heard they were, especially set against the navy walls, but they were mostly empty.

I stayed for another half hour before making my way back to my room, disappointed. The bed had been turned down, and there was a piece of chocolate on the pillow, but it would take a lot more than that to lift my spirits. A lot of towns pulled in the sidewalks early, after all. Not all cities were like New York.

I didn't sleep very well and the next morning woke up early, my body still on New York time. I was hungry though, and decided to order Room Service. But one look at the menu changed that. I'd run out of money before I ever had a chance to make any if I ate any meals here! So I got dressed and went outside to scope out the neighborhood. Before I'd walked more than two or three blocks down State Parkway I happened on a place called O'Connell's on Rush Street. The menu was posted on the window near the entrance, and the prices were reasonable. Things started to look up.

I walked around for awhile after breakfast up to a street called North Avenue, surprised to see one mansion lined up beside the next in what was obviously an upper class neighborhood. Wrought iron fences surrounded many of the properties, which had front yards, something you didn't see much of in New York. I was a few blocks away when I checked my watch. It was almost 9:45! I was meeting a representative from Associated Booking's Chicago office who'd be introducing me to my new orchestra back at the hotel in fifteen minutes! I ran back to the hotel, then up to my room to get the list of songs and key changes, and managed to get back to the front entrance just moments before he pulled up.

"Stanley?" he asked as he stepped out to greet me.

"You must be Hal Munro. Pleased to meet you!" I said, and we shook hands.

"Little young, aren't you?" were his only words to me, a sort of rhetorical question, and we got into the car and drove off toward the Belden Stratford Hotel.

Strange, I thought, that they'd hold it somewhere other than the Ambassador. Truth was they weren't about to let me anywhere near the Pump Room until they could be sure I could handle the job. And my East Coast Society Orchestra turned out to be a group of musicians from Chicago that Associated Booking had put together. There was a trumpet player, a drummer and a bass player, and a guy who played tenor sax and doubled on clarinet. "Little young, aren't you?" was written all over their faces too, but I just ignored it and launched into ". . . a little Cole," as the duchess of Windsor came to mind along with a smile.

"*Night and Day*" I announced, and by the time we got to the second chorus any tension that there'd been had completely evaporated and we were nicely on track.

From my list of a hundred songs we rehearsed forty or fifty of them. When I insisted we move from one song to another, never repeating a second chorus of the same number, band members argued, "People wanna listen to the whole song! We *always* play all the choruses! Whaddaya wanna do somethin' like that for?"

"Because that's the way they do it in New York! *That's* why!" I answered calmly.

I never did let on that I'd just learned the technique myself. Rehearsal continued through late afternoon, and the key changes so carefully thought out on paper came alive when the actual instruments played them. We were all pretty well in sync by the time we finally broke up around four o'clock but I was really nervous. I still had to *think* about each key change instead of moving through them automatically. I wasn't comfortable yet. So I went back to the hotel and asked if there were a room with a piano available anywhere where I could practice.

"The Four Georges is available." they said, and directed me to a banquet room in the Ambassador West.

"Across the street?" I asked, turning back toward the front door.

"Yes . . . or you could take the shortcut through Milsom Street," the girl behind the desk suggested. "That's the tunnel downstairs that connects the two hotels."

I made my way downstairs, while I passed all sorts of little shops on either side of the short passageway, then up another flight of stairs to the Ambassador West. It was decorated differently than the East side, but still looked like it was part of the same place. Same dark paneling everywhere, and well dressed patrons. Elegant. Understated.

I walked through the lobby toward the elevator, past an awning on my right that said The Buttery, and a few minutes later with very little effort had and located the Four Georges Room on the second floor. I sat down at the piano, where I remained till almost midnight, playing every song on my list over and over, checking out all the keys and forcing them into my memory. And that night I slept even less than the one before.

The next morning I met Dr. Nuland downstairs in the lobby. He'd flown in late the night before and had called me, he said. "Out on the town already, eh?" he laughed, and I just smiled, not wanting to admit I was still frantically practicing. We talked about the rehearsal that had taken place the day before, and that Hal Munro had told him we'd gotten off to a "great start," he said.

"At least someone was confident!" I thought, as we climbed into a cab together, on our way to the musician's union hall on West Washington Street. I was a member of a New York local, but I was told that in order to play in Chicago I had to register into "local 10-208." Unions were a pretty serious matter those days, something that didn't have to be explained to musicians or to their managers.

It didn't take long at all, I was pleased to discover, and the next stop was "Wacker and Michigan" he told the next taxi driver, taking us to the London House, Midwestern mecca of jazz musicians, which later became a Burger King. Hal Munro showed up again, along with Chuck Eddy who headed up the Associated Booking Chicago office, and we met for a quick lunch to go over last minute details about my 7:30 opening that night. I hadn't eaten since breakfast the previous day, but was still just too nervous. I stared at the menu for awhile then ordered some coffee, still practicing in my head while I listened to them talk.

After lunch it was back to the Ambassador East, where we'd all meet again at the opening in just a few hours. "Just a few hours!" I kept thinking. I said my good-byes, and as soon as Dr. Nuland was out of sight, ran back through the tunnel and took my place across the street, practicing and practicing and practicing. I was *crazy!* Just after six o'clock I went back over to my room at the Ambassador East to get ready and I think I could have spent the whole night in the shower and never stopped perspiring.

I arrived at the Pump Room an hour early. Gus Kotsais, the maître d', introduced himself. "You look even thinner than you did two nights ago!" he laughed, noticing my expression of "wide eyed terror" was how he'd describe it later. "What you need is a good *dinner*." he suggested, instructing Scotty, the captain, to escort me to the adjacent Parade Room where I was served filet mignon!

The Parade Room ran the full length of the Pump Room, and from where I was sitting I had a pretty good view of the front door and many of the booths. The booths that had been empty only minutes ago were quickly filling with people. By the end of the salad, the room was crowded. As the baked potato disappeared, it was noisy. By 7:30, when the band had gathered, I could feel myself shaking as I stood. My stage presence kicked in pretty quickly though as I walked onto the carpeted stage and greeted my orchestra, then looked around the room and sat down at my piano.

We started with a few medleys—Cole Porter, Gershwin, Jerome Kern, Rodgers and Hart, and for the first ten minutes or so I never once looked up. I just stared at the keys, as though doing so would reduce the risk of disaster. But when I finally relaxed enough to raise my eyes, I could see that people were actually *dancing!* As a matter of fact, the dance floor was *crowded* with couples. And they were smiling! And I was smiling, and for the first time in days, I was really having fun!

Near the end of the first set the place was *jumpin'!* No one seemed to be able to sit still, and neither could I. I stood up at the piano and played the same *Hello Dolly* number I'd done for the Xavier Cugat show in Lisbon, then broke into some Dixieland as a big finale. There was barely room to move on the dance floor now, and everyone in the room was clapping when we finished.

I wasn't nervous at all by the time I made my way through the room through applause toward Frank Gillespie, then the Ambassador's public relations person. "*Great* job!" he said, shaking my hand and putting his arm around my shoulder, then one by one we stopped at each of the white leather booths to greet the guests.

Booth One, closest to the front entrance, was our first stop. Anyone in the room could see whoever it was that was seated there, and vice versa. It was a showcase literally. Irv Kupcinet, the powerful, popular and respected Chicago Sun Times columnist regarded as the Walter Winchell of the Midwest, was seated there beside his wife, Essee. Frank explained that they were the king and queen of social goings on. Irv and Essee could most usually be found in Booth One entertaining visiting celebrities and this booth was in many respects considered theirs.

The next booths on the seating pecking order were the three closest to the front door. These were Booth 11, opposite the entrance with its back against the bar area as it faced the room; Booth 12, directly opposite Booth One and facing it; and Booth 2, directly beside Booth One. Herb Lyon, Chicago Tribune columnist, and his wife Lyle were seated in one of these. Columnist Maggie Daly of the Chicago American was seated in another, with friends Carol Stoll, who would later own the Oak Street Bookstore, Victor Skrebneski, a young photographer then, just coming into his own, and Bruce Gregga, the brilliant young interior designer. Will Leonard, who reviewed the Chicago Tribune music scene, was seated not far away, as were several other people who Frank described as members of the Chicago social scene.

"How long has your orchestra been together?" Will Leonard asked.

I laughed, "Oh, several hours."

He obviously thought I was kidding and insisted, "No really."

"A couple days," I said, the most I could stretch it.

Frank and I stopped at each table over the course of the evening, and I was invited to sit awhile as I joined the guests, answering questions and explaining a little about myself and where I'd come from. I spoke with the Kupcinets and their various guests several times through the course of the night. A remarkable couple, they had a way of putting a stranger like myself completely at ease,

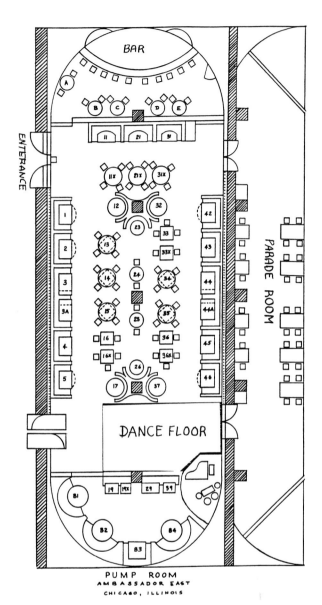

Floor Plan of the original Pump Room.

and within fifteen minutes I think they managed to learn all I ever knew about myself.

"Well, you've been here almost two whole days, any questions we can help you with?" Essee offered.

"Well, I did wonder about one thing," I began. "Do movie stars still come here? I haven't seen many."

"Well . . ." Essee started, "Let me see. Warren Beatty and Leslie Caron were here last weekend.

And Maurice Chevalier just closed at The Empire Room last Saturday night. They come and they go. You just keep playing like you've played tonight and you'll be meeting your fill before very long."

"Not as many as there used to be before the airports, though." Kup added, then explained a little of the room's history. How it was that the movie stars had been drawn here in the first place? "It was the railroad," he began.

Trains were the only way celebrities could travel between Hollywood and New York, and there was always a three to four hour lay over in Chicago. The hotel had limos waiting at the railroad station to pick them up and bring them to the Ambassador. They could freshen up or change before having lunch in the Pump Room, then after lunch they'd take them back to the train station the same way they came. Or they'd spend a night or two, and then leave. Special treatment all the way—including publicity. The press was told who'd be at the Pump Room, so there'd always be some mention of their visit in the papers.

"That much hasn't changed," Essee smiled, looking around. She was right, every paper in the city was represented.

I went back up to the piano and we played several more sets before the night was out, each one with more confidence than the last. It was nearly midnight before the crowd started to die down, and around 1:30 we broke up for the night. Sleepless though I was, resting was the last thing on my mind that magical, triumphant night, so I went upstairs to grab a coat and go out for a walk.

It was cold, and there was a strong wind blowing off the lake, but I hardly felt it. I was invigorated as I walked along, breathing deeper than I'd breathed all week. The neighborhood was quiet, and the streets pretty much deserted, but there were still a few lights here and there. I walked up to Division street then took a right, heading west rather than buck the wind. A bar was still open on the right side of the street called Butch McGuire's, but as I walked on past it seemed like I was the only person outside. And it was nearly 2:30 in the morning when the squad car pulled up and one of the two policemen inside called me over to the curb.

"Whaddaya doin' walkin' around out here?" he asked, and I explained who I was and that I'd just been exploring the neighborhood. But before I finished my second sentence they told me to get in the car.

I was shocked! "Am I being arrested?"

"No," they laughed. "Rescued. You're in Cabrini Green for Christ's sake! Don't be walkin' around here at night!"

And so ended my opening night, the Pump Room's brand new East Coast Society band leader brought home in a squad car!

CHAPTER SIX

STRANGER IN PARADISE

I slept more soundly that night than I had in weeks, and woke up sometime around eleven the next morning. I felt great! I was going to *love* Chicago and I couldn't wait to go out and see some more of it. I got dressed and decided to skip breakfast, then asked the doorman for directions to Marshall Field's. Granted, I was a New Yorker who'd never heard of the Pump Room but *everyone* had heard of Marshall Field's!

"Take the number 36 bus downtown to the loop," he said. "State Street, between Randolph and Washington" and pointed toward the stop

Fifteen minutes later I found myself walking into Field's along with a crowd of hustling, bustling Christmas shoppers. It was the mahogany counters I noticed first. The warm, old world look of it, so different from the sparkling "new remodeled" stores in New York. I wandered from one department to the next for awhile, then got hungry and decided to have a late lunch on the seventh floor at a place called the Walnut Room. It reminded me of service in the best railroad dining car, white linen tablecloths and napkins, and heavy silverware. And there in the center of the room was a spectacularly decorated Christmas tree that just seemed to rise forever.

After lunch I went back down to the main floor, where I was swept away with a group of shop-pers heading out the Wabash exit and onto the sidewalk. And then I saw it.

"Where did *that* come from?" I wondered, looking up for the first time at the elevated. It took awhile to get my bearings, standing there looking up in what was now blustery winter air. Marshall Field's was behind me, literally and figuratively now it was time to find the loop.

"Where's the loop?" I asked a traffic cop working the intersection at Washington.

"You're in it!" he hollered, pointing up and waving his hand around over his head.

The *loop* was everything in the circle that the elevated trains made over this section of the city, I discovered. I took a right on Washington and walked west for awhile, then spotted an interesting store front, with a sign that said "Hillman's" and another that said "Stop 'n Shop." The dazzling displays of food rivaled anything I'd ever seen in New York! I made a mental note to return and took the bus back to my hotel. The moment I got to my room, collapsed on the bed, exhausted.

It was just past seven o'clock that evening when I heard the ringing sound way off in the distance, then suddenly realized it was my telephone! "If you'd like a little dinner before you go on," Gus was suggesting, "you'd better come down right now."

inner! I was playing in half an hour and hadn't even begun to get ready! "Oh . . . thank you very much . . . but . . ." I stammered, doing my best to try to suppress what was utter panic. "I'm in the middle of something right now, but thanks for the offer." And the moment the phone hit the cradle I started rushing around the room like a crazy person and got myself thrown together and onto the stage just as my musicians were starting to worry.

The room was as crowded as it was the previous night, and the music as well received. And during the breaks I visited with people in the booths, just as before. The Kupcinets were in Booth One again and greeted me warmly. Little by little all my apprehensions about leaving New York melted away. When the last customer finally left at about one o'clock in the morning, I joined Gus and Scotty, the unflappablable wait-staff captain, in one of the booths for a late night snack. Before too long, we were talking about the history of the place and the stars who'd been here. Scotty'd been the Pump Room's Head Captain for years, as it turned out, and knew just about everything there was to know about it.

"That was some idea picking movie stars up at the train station in limousines." I said, trying to impress him a little with what I'd already learned, I suppose. "Who thought of that?"

"Why that would have been the owner, Mr. Ernie Byfield. Ever hear of him?"

"Ernie Byfield . . ." I repeated the name slowly. "I heard the name last night, but I don't think I've met him yet. Was he here?"

"Oh, he was here alright!" Scotty laughed. "Just look around . . . he's all over the place! But you didn't meet him last night. And you won't be meetin' him either. He's been dead for years."

"The picture hanging over the bar?" I guessed, wrong again I realized, as the laughter continued.

The Portrait of Beau Nash that adorned the bar.

"Not *that* many years!"

*rnie Byfield, who died nearly fifteen years before, had created the Pump Room at the Ambassador in the 1930s. He modeled it after a place with the same name in a town called Bath, an English resort spa where the upper class took the waters, gambled and gossiped in the early 1700s. Beau Nash was its famous proprietor then, and that's whose picture was hanging over the bar. It was also the reason there was a miniature pump on the wall near the entrance.

Since that night I've heard all sorts of versions of the Pump Room's story, but the most comprehensive appears in a book entitled *Sabers & Suites,* written by Rick Kogan and published in 1983.

"After considering and rejecting dozens of names, he (Byfield) remembered Booth Tarkington's "Monsieur Beauclaire." The setting for this sword-and-dagger adventure was Bath, the 18th century British watering place and gambling spa. Its Pump Room was the first fashionable spot where the aristocracy and actors socialized together. Byfield liked the idea of a place where society would go social climbing after the actors.

"We're going to call it the Pump Room." Byfield told James Hart (his protégé, the dapper general manager of the Ambassadors).

Astounded, Hart said, "We already have a pump room. It's in the basement."

Hart tried to dissuade Byfield from using the Pump Room name. He solicited the opinions of the hotel's permanent guests. Some were so outraged that they threatened to move out of the hotel if the name were used, and one did. Those who stayed drew up a petition imploring Byfield to reconsider.

Undaunted, Byfield hired an amiable local architect named Sam Marx to create his vision, offering hundreds of suggestions, among them the dark blue and white color scheme he had seen at a Lake Forest mansion. Marx set to work. He filled the old entrance with glazed doors and a pump, the latter executed in green and silver. He added crystal chandeliers, a mural of Sarah Siddons, the great 18th century actress, and booths of white leather. A portrait of Nash, painted by Sandor Klein, was hung imposingly above the circular bar.

The Pump Room opened inauspiciously on the night of October 1, 1938. A black-tie supper for the North Avenue Day Nursery attracted a number of local celebrities and Gold Coast socialites. But shortly after the soiree had begun, a nervous headwaiter rushed up to Ernie Byfield.

"There is serious trouble in the kitchen." he said.

"What's the problem?" said Byfield. "Stoves?"

"The waiters are in hiding," said the waiter.

Byfield had originally designed black Court-of-St. James costumes for his waiters, with silk stockings and velvet knee britches. But suddenly deciding that the Pump Room needed color, he switched them into scarlet swallow-tails.

Nothing like this had ever been seen in Chicago before. When the waiters appeared, the kitchen workers greeted them with howls and hooting laughter. The waiters couldn't take it. They ran

A Gentleman in his seventies, being informed that the new restaurant at the Ambassador East was to be named the PUMP ROOM sent the management the following definition from Funk & Wagnalls Unabridged Dictionary

A PUMP
A device for raising, circulating compressing and exhaustng a fluid by drawing or pressing it through apertures
To which he added in parenthesis

(I have such a device)

Private invitation Byfield sent to some of his friends!

out of the kitchen and hid in corridors and closets, certain that the Pump Room customers would greet them with similar derision.

Eventually a few of the bravest waiters ventured into the star-studded fray. The crowd took one look at their outfits . . . and applauded. The costumes were a hit.

"Whatta you guys know, anyway?" the waiters said to the kitchen help. "The swells think we're great."

The laughter subsided. Dinner was served. A number of people got very drunk. And Byfield beamed.

Each booth in the Pump Room became a little stage. Lighting was provided by troughs behind the booths on the side walls and by table lamps that also served as shallow flower bowls. The indirect illumination was quite flattering, removing all lines and shadows from faces. Since Byfield correctly believed that many people came to the Pump Room to be observed by as many observers as possible, he provided 40 little well-staged dramas.

And there was the food, elegant and imaginative: stuffed mushrooms; Chicken Portolla, curried in a coconut shell; Crabmeat ala Byfield; Beef French Market Style; rustafel; imported cheeses; Ice Cream Gertrude Lawrence, a giant rum cake shaped like a pump and Strawberries Booth One.

One waiter only served curry.

Fabulous food displays.

"I don't want grim gourmets around my restaurants," Byfield said. "I want laughing eaters."

He provided quite a show—waiters clad in hunting red swallow-tailed coats, the coffee boy garbed in emerald with a white satin turban plumed with ostrich feathers and the curry boy dressed in deep gold.

There were wagons of all kinds: hors d'oeuvre wagons, chafing-dish wagons, roast wagons, pastry wagons, cheese wagons, fruit wagons, cold soup wagons, curry wagons. Some were heated and some heaped with ice sculpted into bizarre shapes. When anyone ordered

There were wagons of all kinds.

The Pump Room's traveling food show.

roast pheasant, the finished bird arrived completely clad in its original plumage. This traveling food show, a prime example of Byfield's showmanship, was actually a cagey way of keeping some foods hot, since the kitchen was located one floor below.

The most spectacular food display was the flaming sword dishes. With a ceremonious display of pyrotechnics that make Greek restaurant hoopla over flaming saganaki look positively tame, Pump Room waiters flamed a variety of dishes table side. The entrance was quite dramatic, and all eyes turned to peruse the waiters' adroitness. Most of the flaming dishes were ordered by out-of-town visitors. One inventive—or tipsy—guest began a dinner party with 12 ripe olives brought in on 12-inch long brochettes by 12 waiters.

"It doesn't hurt the food—much." Byfield said often. "We serve almost anything flambé in that room, occasionally even a waiter's thumb."

Actually, there is considerable evidence that Byfield may have considered the Pump Room a grand practical joke. A satire on pretentiousness. He'd come to an interesting conclusion: The old families were on their way out of the social limelight; Hollywood stars and bathing beauties were in. And if they weren't he'd provide a little push.

"It doesn't hurt the food—much." Ernie Byfield.

On October 10, 1938, nine days after opening his Ambassador East spa, one of Byfield's many celebrated friends walked into the Pump Room. When she finally left, after spending each late evening there for the next 90 days, the room's repute was forever established.

Gertrude Lawrence, the distinguished actress, was then starring in "Susan and God" at the Harris Theater. Every night after her performance, she showed up at the Pump Room and held court in a booth located just to the right of the entrance. Whether coerced there by Byfield's pleas or genuinely taken with the room, Gertrude Lawrence gave the room its first dose of certifiable celebrity.

Gertrude Lawrence.

Just plain folks flocked to see where she sat, other stars joined her court, society matrons began peeking at her from their tables and the mystique of Booth One was started. The theatrical sit-in earned Miss Lawrence eternal Pump Room gratitude. A special plaque reserved the table for her whenever she was in town and another one kept the table empty for a week after she died.

The Pump Room

SUMMER COOLERS

Tom Collins 50	French (75's) 1.25	Sloe Gin Blossom 50
Mint Collins 65	Summer Breeze 65	Floradora 65
Pump Room Daisy 60	Hawaiian Cooler 85	Cubano Dream 65

DRINK SPECIALTIES

The Bath Cure (Only One to a Guest) 1.00

Champagne Cocktail 85	Frozen Daiquiri 60
Dagger Palm Punch 90	Planter's Punch 90
Russian Tom 65	Mint Julep 90

COCKTAILS

Ambassador 50	Alexander 50	Bacardi 50
Bronx 50	Cloverleaf 50	Daiquiri 50
Dubonnet 50	Martini 40	Manhattan 50
Old Fashion 50	Perfect 50	Pink Lady 50
Sazerac 50	Stinger 50	Side Car 50
	Coffee Alexander 65	

Sours 50 & 60   Fizzes 50 & 60   Flips 50 & 60   Highballs 50 & 60

WINES

CHAMPAGNE

	Bottle	½ Bottle
Louis Roederer Brut—1928	7.50	4.00
Clicquot Yellow Label	7.00	3.75
Clicquot Yellow Label—1928	7.50	4.00
Mumm's Extra Dry	7.00	3.75
Mumm's Cordon Rouge—1928	8.00	4.25
Lanson—1928	7.50	4.00
Charles Heidsieck—1928	7.50	4.00
Pol Roger—1926	8.50	4.50
Dry Monopole	7.00	3.75
Dry Monopole—1928	7.50	4.00
Ernest Irroy—1928	7.50	4.00
Ernest Irroy—1926	8.00	4.25

AMERICAN CHAMPAGNE

Cook's Imperial	4.50	3.00

BORDEAUX (WHITE)

Sauternes—1929—Cruse & Fils	3.25	2.00
Haut Sauternes—1934—Sichel	3.25	2.00
Chateau Latour Blanche—1929—Eschenauer	3.75	2.25
Chateau Yquem—1929—Eschenauer	5.50	

BORDEAUX (RED)

Chateau Fontet Canet—1934—Cruse & Fils	3.25	2.00
Chateau Margaux—1934—Eschenauer	3.75	2.25
Chateau Latour—1923—Eschenauer	4.25	2.50
Chateau Leoville—1929—Cruse & Fils	4.25	2.50

BURGUNDY (WHITE)

Meursault—1926—Chanson	3.25	
Chablis—1928—Cruse & Fils	3.75	2.25
Montrachet—1928—Chanson	4.25	

BURGUNDY (RED)

Pommard—1923—Eschenauer	3.25	
Pommard—1926—Cruse & Fils	3.75	2.25
Chambertin—1926—Chanson	4.25	
Gevry Chambertin—1928—Cruse & Fils	4.25	2.50

SPARKLING BURGUNDY

Barton & Guestier	5.75	3.25
Chauvenet Red Cap	6.75	3.75

COGNACS

Sherman House Cellars....50	Hennessy's Three Star....50	
Metaxa 50	Martells....50	Courvoisier....60
	Remy Martin....50	

FLAMING SWORD DINNER
$3.00

Choice of:

Clam or Tomato Juice Cocktail Frappe
Fresh Fruit Cocktail
Antipasto
Filet of Herring with Sour Cream
or
Soup on Wagon
———
Relish in Bowl
———

Choice of:

Shashlick, Caucasian Rissoto
Jumbo Squab a la Broche
Chicken Livers, Talleyrand
Scallops, Mushrooms, Bacon
en Brochette
Mignon of Pork Tenderloin
au Champignon
Tenderloin of Beef Rossini (50c extra)

———
Tomato Brochette
———
Potatoes du Jour
———
Salad on Wagon
———
Dessert on Wagon
———
Coffee

JOHN KIRBY
AND HIS BAND
PLAYS FOR
SUPPER DANCING
9:30 P. M. to CLOSING

COCKTAIL HOUR
DANCING
SATURDAY & SUNDAY
4:30 TO 6:30 P. M.

SPECIAL SUNDAY
ENGLISH BREAKFAST
SERVED FROM
TWELVE NOON
ONE DOLLAR

Specialties of The Pump Room *and Delicacies in Season*

DINNER

ON THE SHELL
Bluepoints 60   Cotuits 60   Little Necks 60   Cherrystones 60
Baked Clams Casino 1.00   Oyster Stew, Milk 75; Half and Half 90; Cream 1.00

APPETIZERS
Tartar Stuffed Celery 60   Grapefruit Juice 30   Half Grapefruit 35   **Clam Juice Frappe 30**   Antipasto 40
Tomato Juice Cocktail Frappe 30   Fruit Cocktail 45   **Filets of Herring with Sour Cream 50**   **Shrimp Cocktail 50**
Chopped Chicken Livers 45   Stuffed Celery 60   Supreme of Fresh Fruit au Kirsch 65
Crabmeat Cocktail 65   Crabmeat Canape (Hot) 75   Hors d'Oeuvers Tray 90   Fresh Lobster Cocktail 1.00
French Fan Fried Shrimps, Tempura 60   **Baked Jumbo Shrimps, Mignonette 60**

SOUPS
Fresh Vegetable Soup .... 30 (On Wagon)   Essence of Black Mushrooms au Chablis 35 (On Wagon)
Cream of Tomato 30   Consomme Xavier 30
                          Chicken Cuban Carola 35

FRESH FROM THE LAKES AND SEA
Broiled Live Lobster, Julienne Potatoes 2.00   Cracked California Crab, Mustard Mayonnaise 1.75
Broiled Lake Superior Jumbo Whitefish, Maitre d'Hotel 1.40   Lobster Thermidor 2.25
Fresh Pompano au Beurre Noir 1.40   Broiled Live Lobster, Julienne Potatoes 2.00
                          Jumbo Frog Legs Saute, Almondine 1.40

THE CHEF HAS PREPARED SPECIALLY
Roast Young Bronze Turkey, Chestnut Dressing, Fresh Cranberry Sauce 1.50
Roast Prime Rib of Beef au Jus, Yorkshire Pudding 1.50
Sliced Chicken and Sweetbreads, Toulouse, Supreme Sauce .... 1.85 (On Wagon)
Boiled Brisket of Honey Cured Corned Beef and Cabbage, Boiled Potato 1.50
Planked Salisbury Steak, Jardiniere, Bordelaise Sauce 1.50
Baked Oysters Louisiana (Stuffed with Crabmeat au Gratin) 1.45

DISHES HIGHLY SEASONED WITH GARLIC
Fresh Lobster 2.25   Jumbo Shrimps 1.50   Fresh Jumbo Frog Legs 1.50   Escargots Bourguignonne 1.35

CURRIES
                          Pilaff of Chicken Minaret 1.75
Half of Chicken, Unjointed, Calcutta, Avocado Pear 1.75   **Fresh Shrimps with Rice and Kumquats 1.60**
Curry of Lamb, Chutney, Alexandria 1.60   **Chicken, Portolla, Cooked and Served in a Cocoanut 1.75**

DEVILED DISHES
Chopped Deviled Prime Sirloin Steak, Beau Nash 1.50   Deviled Roast Beef, Bienville 1.50
Deviled Breast of Chicken, Sanford 1.50   Baked Giant Deviled Crab 1.50

CHAFING DISHES
Creamed Capon on Buttered Noodles au Gratin 1.75   Fresh Crabflakes, Feodora 1.75
Chicken and Lobster, Madeira Wine, Rice, Kumquats 1.85   Fresh Lobster, Newburg 2.25
Chicken a la King 1.75   Poached Half of Fresh Dressed Chicken a la Ritz 1.50

FLAMING BROCHETTES
Jumbo Squab a la Broche 1.85   Whole Squab Chicken 1.85   **Chicken Livers, Talleyrand 1.60**
Shashlick Caucasian 1.85   Tenderloin of Beef, Rossini 2.50   Double Lamb Chop, Mixed Grill 1.75
                 Scallops, Mushrooms, Bacon en Brochette 1.65

FROM OUR HICKORY CHARCOAL GRILL ALL OUR BEEF IS U. S. PRIME
                                  Prime Sirloin Steak 2.75
Whole Roast Rainbow Farm Pheasant (for 2) 4.50 en Plumage 5.00 (45 min.)   Spring Lamb Chops 1.40
Genuine Mallard Duck, Roasted with Wild Rice (for 2) 3.00 (25 minutes) or Split and Broiled, Half 1.75; Whole 3.00
Split Minute Sirloin Steak Saute, Cottage Fried Potatoes 2.25   Beef Tenderloin with Mushrooms 2.50

FRESH FROM THE GARDEN
Cottage Fried Potatoes 50   Grilled Fresh Tomatoes 45   **Green Asparagus Hollandaise 40**
Hashed Brown, Candied Sweet, Mashed or Boiled Potato 25   Stewed Fresh Tomatoes 25
Broccoli Hollandaise 40   French Peas, Paysanne 30   Creamed Celery 25

SALADS, STUFFED AVOCADOS, TOMATOES
French Endive, Banana and Grapes, French Dressing 35
Crisp Lettuce, Roquefort Cheese Dressing 50   Chicken and Fresh Vegetable Salad 1.25
Pump Room Bowl (on Wagon) 50   Fresh Fruit, Pump Room Dressing 75   Giant White Asparagus Vinaigrette 90
Avocado Pear Filled with Fresh Crabmeat or Shrimps 1.35   Tomato Stuffed with Chicken Salad 1.35

PASTRIES, FRUITS, ICE CREAMS, AND FLAMING DESSERTS
French Apple Pie 25   Fresh Plum or Lemon Meringue Pie 30   Caramel Pecan Rum Cake 35
Baba au Rum 25   Macaroon Slice 30   **Parfait Nordica 45**
Orange, Raspberry, Lemon or Pineapple Ice 30   **French Pastry 30**   Chocolate Ice Cream, Bermuda 75
Coffee Ice Cream, Creme de Mocha 65   Vanilla Ice Cream, Sauce Lawrence 65
Peach, French Vanilla, Chocolate, Strawberry or Pink Peppermint Stick Ice Cream 35   Crepes Suzette 1.25
Fruit Compote (On Wagon) 50   **Your Favorite Cheese (On Wagon)**   Stilton in Port Wine 65
Compote of Fruit au Fum 75   Berries in Season with Cream 45   Black Cherries, Flambe 90
Milk 25   Tea 25   Sanka 25   Cafe Diable 50   Ambassador Blend Coffee 20
Special Sumatra Coffee 25   Iced Tea or Coffee 25   Assorted Rolls, Bread and Butter 10

A Young Frank Sinatra whirls Essee Kupcinet to David LeWinter's Orchestra mid 1940s.

Gloria Swanson was either intrigued by one of Ernie Byfield's stories, or she was ready to nod off?

Bogie and Bacall on their honeymoon at the hotel.

The day the Queen came to lunch. "I had stories running everywhere for weeks before her arrival," remembered Perrigo. "Things like whether American or French wines should be served and how to dress a suite for a Queen?" There was a tremendous amount of excitement. After all the celebrities, Queen Elizabeth really did it to me. "She showed up dressed heavily in white lace. She looked like a Red Cross nurse. She had been sick, so she looked all one color."

Will the real Eddie Cantor standup?

Eleanor Roosevelt was interviewed in the Parade Room by budding newswoman Ann Gerber.

The newlyweds-Robert Wagner and Natalie Wood.

Chicago loved Lucy and Desi when they visited the hotel.

June Allison and husband Dick Powell.

Cyd Charisse and Tony Martin celebrate their wedding at the Pump Room.

Judy Garland with her children Liza Minnelli, Joey and Lorna Luft.

Nancy Davis Reagan and Carol Channing compare baby photos in booth one.

From left to right: James Hart, Founder of Sarah Siddons Society, Dorothy Siddons Lasher, Great, Great, Great Grandaughter of Sarah Siddons, Actress Bea Lillie, Frank W. Bering, Chairman of the Board of the Sherman-Ambassador Hotels, Eugene E. Barrett Vice President of the Hotel.

Child star Margaret O'Brien putting on her first lipstick in booth one.

Lucia Perrigo said when Bea Lillie was presented with her award, she slid right into the fireplace after a few too many cocktails.

The famous hotelman Conrad Hilton with girlfriend Ann Miller and new daughter-in-law Elizabeth Taylor in booth one (1950).

The King, Clark Gable, thrilled Essee Kupcinet with a hug.

Booth one late 1940s. From left to right; Frank Sinatra, Janice Paige, Kup, Jane Russell, Peter Lawford, Essee Kupcinet and some fans being served by composer Jules Styne who donned a waiters jacket.

Joan Crawford and new husband Alfred M. Steele brawled at their wedding breakfast moments after this somewhat happy photo was taken.

Sarah Siddons Walk

Dedicated to the gifted Sarah, England's immortal 18th century actress who frequented the original Pump Room. The Sarah Siddons Walk provides a garden setting for private parties. Its celebrated illusion wall evokes the atmosphere of a vast formal garden.

The Buttery

is as English in tradition and taste as the collegiate Butteries of Britain's universities where students and dons congregate for refreshment. Forerunner of all the dining rooms in the Hotels Ambassador, its opening set a unique style in fabulous dining, flaming swords and wagon service. A magnet for both smart young society and theatrical luminaries, the Buttery, with its sophisticated music and Tartan-clad servitors, is open daily for luncheon, cocktails, dinner and supper. Reservations are advised.

Newlyweds Eddie Fisher and Elizabeth Taylor.

Alan Ladd and wife Sue Carroll.

The Parade

The Parade, adjacent to the Pump Room and having a similar luxurious atmosphere, was named after the promenade which encircled the original Pump Room of Bath, England. Available by special arrangement for luncheon, cocktail, dinner and supper parties.

ut 90 days do not make an institution and Byfield and his staff had to work incessantly to make Booth One The Place for Important Persons. Byfield wanted a restaurant that would be like a theater with Booth One taking the place of the stage. He pointed out that the English Pump Room was the first place where society deigned to mingle with actors, and that the Chicago Pump Room was where performers deigned to mingle with society.

And Jack Benny, who once said, The Pump Room is the only dining room in the world where I do not mind eating alone. Even the bus boys talk to me," didn't miss a beat when presented one evening with ice cubes flambé: "They'll serve everything on a flaming sword except the check."

Lucia Perrigo, the Ambassador's tireless and inventive publicist for nearly 30 years, said it perfectly: "People have done everything in Booth One except be born."

During Byfield's lifetime, some of the visitors included Archduke of Austria, Sir Cedric Hardwick, Dale Carnegie, Eleanor Roosevelt, Laurence Olivier, Helena Rubenstein, Richard Rogers, Sinclair Lewis, Claire Booth, Cornelius Vanderbilt, Jr., Cornelia Otis Skinner, John Steinbeck, and Orson Welles.

By the time I went to sleep that night I felt like a part of living history and I liked it.

When the reviews came out in each of the city's four newspapers the following week-end, everything was so positive I couldn't believe it!

> Irv Kupcinet, Kup's Column, Chicago Sun Times: "Maestro Stan Paul can take a bow for the new sounds in the Pump Room. His music is delightful."

> Herb Lyon, Tower Ticker, Chicago Tribune, Monday December 7, 1964: "New pianner player in town, Stan Paul, is a quick click as Pump Room maestro; he ripples away much like a young Eddie Duchin."

> Will Leonard, On the Town, Chicago Tribune weekend edition, Sunday, December 6, 1964: "Stanley Paul's Music Joy to Ears and Feet: The Pump Room has the youngest band leader in its history, and the sound and the atmosphere around the dance floor in the Ambassador East are new and different. Stanley Paul, still in his twenties, is a piano man with a ringing tone, a striding tempo, a supple torso that bends back and forth with every bar, and a good will that transmits itself to the dancers. This is another "society" orchestra from the east, in theory, but it's really Mr. Paul and accompanists. Asked by a reporter how long this band has been together, Stanley replied truthfully and disarmingly, "About two days." The sidemen are four good local lads who prove again what capable members the musicians' union has in these parts–and Stanley's arrangements are great, swinging, melodious jobs that are a joy to the ear as well as the foot. This should be a happy winter season in the Pump Room."
>

Soon there was a mention of the band in one column or another just about every day. And it wasn't long before I was getting calls to do interviews! One question I seem to have been asked more than any other was "How do you like Chicago compared to New York?" One thing's for certain, I'd never been noticed like this in New York! But there were a million things about the city that I loved, and I'd just gotten here. I was having a ball!

Randolph Street looking east there were fabulous movie palaces all over the loop.

I soon discovered the subway at Clark and Division, just a few blocks from the Ambassador, and rode it to catch a movie downtown whenever I had a chance. There were fabulous movie palaces all over the Loop, each different yet all somehow alike. State Street had the Chicago, the State Lake and the Roosevelt, the McVickers was on Madison, and on Randolph there was the Woods, the United Artists, that fabulous Oriental and the Palace. I really got a kick out of those garish Balaban & Katz confections.

I loved the neighborhood around the Ambassador Hotel. I'd walk the few blocks to the lake, which was so different from New York. In Chicago, the lake was open instead of crowded by piers and buildings. I hoped I would still be here in the summer, when I might enjoy the unique experience of having a beach within walking distance of where I lived—another vast difference from New York.

Then I'd walk to the grand, old Drake Hotel at the corner of Oak Street and Michigan Avenue. I used to love to go to the Drake's drug store, which I remember had the best chicken salad sandwiches in the world. I still miss sitting at the counter, but for the life of me I can't remember what was the secret of those terrific sandwiches.

After that, I might walk one block south to Walton and stop at Mrs. Snyder's, which was the place for chocolate milk shakes and hot fudge sundaes. Being so young, I'd burn off all the desserts I wanted just by walking a couple of miles down Michigan Avenue to the Wrigley Building and back again. How wonderful were the days of desserts without guilt.

Michigan Avenue was quaint in those days, with smaller shops and low-rise buildings. Among the taller structures was the Palmolive Building, where the Lindbergh Beacon rotated every night, the Allerton Hotel, where Don McNeill's Breakfast Club was broadcast from the Tip Top Tap every weekday morning, and the Tribune Tower, which was supposed to look like an English King's throne. There was also Blum's Vogue, Sak's Fifth Avenue (which was across the street from its present location), Stanley Korshak, Bonwit Teller, Charmet's Restaurant, where students of the modeling school upstairs stopped for coffee, and so many other now-disappeared emporiums.

At a time when a woman's hat was an important part of her wardrobe, Bes Ben was the place for fancy women's hats. It was presided over by Benjamin Green-Field, who was a Chicago treasure. I had heard the stories about his amazing hat sales, which drew Lake Forest matrons to the Drake for an overnight stay so they would be on hand near dawn when Green-Field would stand on a ladder and throw out his 'hundred-dollar-and up' hats for $5 each.

Other afternoons, I might walk to Oak Street, which had a warm sophistication about it. A favorite hangout of mine was an antique store called Callard's of London. Mr. Callard would

(Chicago Historical Society photo)

Corner of Michigan Ave and Oak St. Looking from right to left, Martha Weathered, Anna's Florist, Trabert and Hoeffer, Bes-Ben, Hollands Gallery, Mrs. Snyders, Next block *Blums Vogue, Jacques, Stanley Korshak.*

spend hours explaining English antiques and silver, even though I couldn't afford to buy anything. I was an eager student.

I'd stroll a few doors from Callard's where I'd eat lunch in the back of a drug store called Musket and Henriksen. If they could have just franchised their egg salad sandwiches, Musket and Henriksen might still be in existence to this day.

Oak Street also boasted Eli's Delicatessen, where the owner always said he remembered the first day I came in. According to Eli, I ordered "a corned beef sandwich with coleslaw, Russian dressing and a vanilla egg cream, please." Then I asked him how could he tell I was from New York?

It wasn't long before my explorations led me to Maxwell Street, Chicago's flea market paradise. Sometimes I'd finish work at the Pump Room around three o'clock in the morning on a Saturday night, grab a couple hours' sleep and be down there by 7 a.m. looking for treasures. I think the doorman at the hotel thought I was nuts, continually bringing all these strange finds in through the revolving doors. While most of the guests would be carrying shopping bags from Marshall Fields or Saks, you could find Stanley Paul completely covered with dust, shlepping a wind up phonograph with a horn no less!

At the time, the Old Town area was growing "increasingly popular" people said, so I wandered over that way one day. It reminded me of Greenwich Village. I loved it! The Second City troupe was offering impromptu comedy, always different and a guaranteed hit. There were great hamburgers at Chances Are and the Pickle Barrel, complete with peanut shells on the floor, and terrific steaks at That Steak Joint, served in a comfortable saloon atmosphere. And I often wandered into a little shop on Wells Street that had opened the year before called Crate and Barrel.

I hadn't been at the Pump Room for more than a couple weeks before I started getting invitations to join customers for dinner on my nights off! They were people from the neighborhood who'd stop in several times a week, sometimes for dinner and sometimes for a drink at the bar after dining at another restaurant. People were easy to get to know. They were friendly, inviting me to join them at their table and asking a million questions about me and New York. It was almost as though I were a celebrity or something myself.

In those years, clubs that featured dining were the rage. We'd go to places like Club Boyer, The Key Club, The Barclay, or the Whitehall, famous for its Steak Diane. And the view from the Mid America Club! It was located on top of the Prudential building then, which in those years was one of the tallest buildings in Chicago.

A wonderful restaurant called Jacques stood at the corner of Delaware and Michigan Avenue, where Bloomingdales is now. What I most remember was its garden setting with a glass ceiling that let you sit beneath falling snow flakes or raindrops, comfortable and watching the weather from the inside. The Cafe de Paris on Dearborn Street was famous for duck. Don the Beachcomber on Walton Street was run by a man called Pinky who always wore a white tuxedo. And across the street from the Ambassador at the Churchill Hotel were Maison Lafite and Mon Petit, where Norman Wallace was featured at the piano.

That very first dinner invitation I received is the one that's unforgettable, though, and not just because it was the first. It was the end of the second week. A couple I'd seen at the Pump Room on several occasions had asked me to join them at their table a few times, which was always Booth 37, just off the dance floor near the bandstand. After about three or four evenings like this, they offered to "show me the town."

I later mentioned it to Scotty, the wait-staff captain, and his face got a strange expression as he said he'd heard they were in the drug business. I thought nothing more about it, and the following Monday night this big black limo pulled up to the hotel and I was whisked off to my first big night on the town. His wife was wearing just about the biggest diamond ring I'd ever seen and she was wrapped in a coat that had to have been sable, and I remember thinking "These people are really wealthy!"

They were going to one of their favorite restaurants, Frank and Marie's, which was up on Sheridan Road near the Edgewater Beach Hotel. Not for a second did we ever seem to run out of anything. Champagne, caviar, lobster—the works! And I'd never seen anyone hand out tips like this guy did in my life—twenty dollar bills, and an occasional fifty! And remember this was 1964. Then after the entree, he announced that we were leaving to have dessert at another restaurant! So we climbed into the waiting limo and headed back toward downtown, pulling up in front of the Imperial House on Walton Street, where he ordered something called chocolate snowballs for all of us, which, as I recall, were marvelous.

Just as things seemed to be winding down, we were on our way out the door, going "clubbing" our host insisted. On and on we went, to one club after another, and wherever we went those huge tips just kept on coming. I was at a loss for words most of the night, but I think it was at Adolph's on Rush Street that I finally opened my mouth. "Before tonight I never realized that drugs could be such a great business! Which drug stores are yours?" I asked.

They never said a word, just stared at each other and then at me. Within five minutes or so I found myself whisked back to the hotel. How was I supposed to know what kind of drug business they were in? Funny, we never did see that couple in the Pump Room again.

As weeks went by I was developing a growing circle of acquaintances, and had all sorts of oppor-

tunities to meet movie stars. I saw Joan Crawford, Alfred Lunt and Lynn Fontaine. Joan Bennett and her sister Constance, but I remember they sat in separate booths. Maybe they didn't get along?

Every time I would get on the elevator, I would have to stop myself from gawking and making a fool out of myself. Standing there might be Frank Sinatra, Robert Kennedy, Helen Hayes, Joe DiMaggio or someone I had just seen on the cover of Time Magazine the week before!

Bob Elson with Constance Bennett. He had a daily radio show from the Pump Room. Many times I would get a frantic phone call from Mr. Elson, "Get right down here, I need you." That was a sign that one of his famous guests hadn't shown up.

Then finally, in the ninth week of the engagement, the manager, John Bogardus, invited me to his office. "Stanley, I gotta tell you, you've done a terrific job here," he began, walking around his desk and slowly dropping into his big leather chair. "No one could possibly have predicted that you'd do so well!"

"Thank you!" I beamed, and settled in a little. He went on and on about how well I'd done, how well received I'd been, and then mentioned how complicated the entertainment industry could be. "Oops!" I'm thinking. "Did I miss something?" And then . . .

"There's nothin' to do but come right out and say it. Stanley, we won't be extending your contract. Thirteen weeks, that's it. We've got another band leader who'll be taking your place in March."

I was flash frozen. I couldn't believe what I'd just heard, but I was too shocked to ask a single question! He came out from behind his desk and escorted me to the door, offering no further explanation. I went directly to my room and called Associated Booking. They told me that Mr. Bogardus had called and given them the word that morning. Apparently, before I was hired he'd signed with Chauncey Grey, a well-known society band leader from New York. I'd heard of him, even seen him play. He'd been the orchestra leader at the El Morocco for years, and had appeared at quite a few of the city's other top clubs. He couldn't start any earlier than mid-February, so they hired me as filler but they never told me. They never told anyone. They never considered that the kid they hired might be such a hit. Nobody did! And while the success complicated things, they had a signed contract with Chauncey and they had to let me go.

I was disappointed, but I was angry too! Word was out later that day. Herb Lyon, from the Tribune, called and asked why I was leaving. I really didn't know what to say to him. I was too embarrassed by the whole thing. Embarrassed . . . and looking for work in New York.

CHAPTER SEVEN

TWISTS OF FATE

I returned to New York early in March with few prospects. I'd been calling Associated Booking almost daily, but no one was hiring. It was the mid sixties, the Dawning of the Age of Aquarius, and the trend away from dance bands continued. The hotels which, once upon a time, had an orchestra or two, were phasing them out, one by one. Even the night clubs were shuttered, the pianos and horns quieted, and the musicians were standing in the unemployment lines. I was collecting about $50 a week and still making daily calls to my agent and many others, as a matter of fact. Finally, after what seemed like a long search, I got job, a one-nighter at a joint called Florence's Pin Up Room.

The room bore a striking resemblance to the bar in Philadelphia where I'd first played for Sally Rand. It was a dive. It was seedy. I didn't want to be there, but it was all I could get. I was miserable but, swallowing my pride, I sat down at the piano and started to play. When I was about six bars into the song, a heavy hand suddenly clamped on my left shoulder. The hand was attached to a big burly fellow who menacingly said, "You don't have a contract. You can't play here." This representative of the musicians' union combined the toughness of Humphrey Bogart with the size of a piano mover—not a man to take lightly, much less ignore.

It was a scene from a bad B movie, and it was mine, which made it that much worse. I was physically escorted from the piano, and deposited at the bar. I sat down, and stared at my image in the mirrored walls behind the liquor bottles. I looked terrible and I felt worse. "You gonna be drinkin' or what?" the bartender asked… and I ordered a scotch.

"Make that a *double*," I said, then downed it and promptly threw up.

This was the lowest point I'd ever reached in my career. Quite a fall from 'East Coast Society Orchestra Leader' in the Pump Room to playing at Florence's Pin Up Room and being physically removed from the piano bench!

After that, I tried to keep as busy as possible and battled to be optimistic rather than down-hearted. Only a few days later, fate intervened! I got a call about an opening at a new night club in North Bergen, New Jersey. It was located off a truck stop near the Lincoln Tunnel. I had no idea why anyone would want to build anything way out there but a diner or a tattoo parlor. It wasn't New York, but they wanted an orchestra and I was an "orchestra leader" after all, wasn't I? So I seized the opportunity and got a small orchestra together, pronto.

The Chateau Renaissance was its name, and it looked like a cross between Mama Leone's Italian Restaurant and Loew's 86th Street Movie Palace. Fake marble was everywhere, and the walls featured Roman street scenes coyly back lighted. It was an ersatz set gone wrong—as wrong as the Pump Room had been right. However it was here in this unlikely, out of the way place that I first made the acquaintance of one Miss Bette Davis!

A few weeks before my appearance there, Miss Davis had been on her way back to New York from Philadelphia, where she'd been a guest on the Mike Douglas TV Show. She got stranded en route by the great New York City blackout—you remember, the one where the birth rate soared nine months later? She saw the sign for the Chateau Renaissance, which was a combined nightclub and roadside motel. She pulled in with her manager, Viola Rubber. Yes, that was her name, as in the tree.

As luck would have it, she became absolutely smitten with the manager at the Chateau who was at least a decade younger than she was, a fact that didn't seem to bother her one bit. By the time I opened, the film legend had become a regular at the club.

Bette Davis was in the midst of a career renaissance, of sorts. She starred in *Whatever Happened to Baby Jane?*, with Joan Crawford as her screen nemesis, and *Hush, Hush, Sweet Charlotte*, a cinemagraphic potboiler which also featured Olivia DeHavilland and which she told me had financed her daughter B.D.'s wedding.

I met her during my first night. I was playing a dance set and Miss Davis sent a note to me to join her and her party when I finished.

"Where did you *e-vah* learn to play the pi-a-no like that?" were her first words.

"My God, she really does talk like that!" I thought. We immediately began comparing stories of how each of us wound up in North Bergen, New Jersey.

"But Stanleypaul," she said, "you will nevah go anywhere if you do not *sing* the ly-rics to those songs!" What a boost it would be to my career, she insisted. And she was serious. Very serious it seemed to me.

"How fortunate I am!" I kept thinking as I was offered career advice from one of the world's greatest stars! All this time as a musician and the prospect of *singing* had not once crossed my mind! I was inspired.

There was no time like the present to get started, so on the way back to New York that evening, I gave

The night I met her, she signed this photo, "Sing-Sing-Sing." Unfortunately, I followed her advice!

it a try while my bass player drove. I sang and sang and sang, until right smack in the middle of the Lincoln Tunnel, he screamed "Stanley, will you please *shut the hell up!* You can't *sing!* You sound *terrible!*"

"What does he know, anyway," I thought. "Peter Duchin doesn't sing. I could very well be the only society band leader in the United States who sings! Maybe I'll become a singing sensation in Las Vegas!" I'd envisioned another twenty fabulous scenarios by morning, when I started calling everyone I knew to see if any of them could suggest a good vocal coach for me.

The name Coe Glade came up a few times. Later that week I went to see her for my first lesson. Her studio was in an old apartment building around 72nd Street on the west side, the kind that opera singers lived in during those years. Miss Glade had been the diva who'd sung *Carmen* at Radio City Music Hall's opening in 1932. Now, a vision of her former self, with outstretched flaps of operatic arms, she still had Carmen's comb firmly in her slicked-back, black-shoe-polish hair. She sang not *Carmen*, not *Rigoletto*, but scales!

I became a devoted student and practiced singing loud and confidently every waking moment. My piano was near a window, and every once in awhile you could hear a neighbor's window slamming shut, and a few of the more ardent neighborhood critics hurled expletives and threats. But nothing could stop me! Especially when I received a letter from *the Legend* herself.

So with all this encouragement and ceaseless practicing, after only three weeks I decided I was ready to make my singing debut. I called Viola Rubber to find out where I could reach my mentor Miss Davis to tell her that I was ready for all the world to hear me.

A few days later Miss Davis was on the phone asking, "Are you any *good*, Stanleypaul? Are you *prac*-tisss-ing?" Then she told me she'd come see me in a few weeks, when she finished filming on the coast.

In the interim, I drove my neighbors nearly crazy, and bragged to friends, family, even employees in the restaurant about my "upcoming triumph in blending two musical arts." Finally, to everyone's relief, the big night arrived. I was on stage when I noticed that Bette Davis and her party had arrived.

About twenty minutes later I saw her gesturing wildly that she was ready for the big moment! I burst, and I do mean burst, into my own enthusiastic version of Enzio Pinza's *Some Enchanted Evening*. Eyes widened. Patrons in the restaurant looked at each other with raised eyebrows. The waiters stopped serving as graveyard silence descended over the restaurant.

And Miss Davis? She was doubled over laughing! Her response surged to a howl when the manager of the club advised me, "Stick to the piano, Paul." As I approached her table after my debut singing recital, she shouted "*Well . . . may*-be that wa-sn't such a good i-de-a af-ter *all*. The peo-

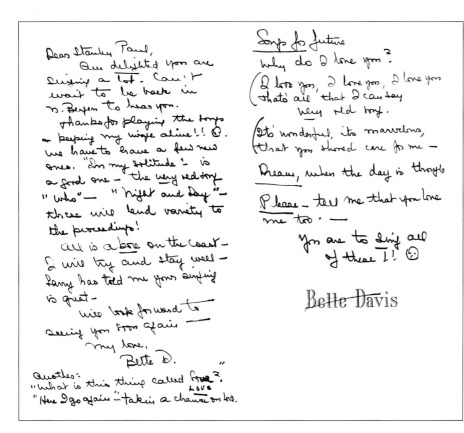

ple will just have to *think* the words, Stanleypaul. You just *play*!"

We became friends. Any time Bette Davis was there, it was a given that I'd sit with her. One night, about a week later, I'd joined her and a group of her friends at her table between sets. As usual, she was in the middle of a gigantic cloud of smoke, with the usual two open packs of Chesterfield cigarettes sitting near her on the table. God forbid they should run out! The table beside us was filled with a dozen jolly conventioneers, drinking, eating steak, pestering her for autographs and extending endless invitations to her to join them at their table. They were getting drunk. And they were getting louder.

After about fifteen minutes of aggravation, she whispered, "Watch *this* . . ." and got up from the table. She reached into her handbag and brought out a huge perfume atomizer. "You *wan*-ted a momento?" she asked sweetly.

"Yes!" they screamed. That was when she sprayed each of the men individually with a big poof!

"There you *are* then! Go home and tell your wives that *Bette Davis* sprayed you with cologne in North Bergen!" she said as their table got very quiet. She let them squirm awhile, wondering how they'd get their wives to believe their aromas belonged to Bette Davis, of all people. Or that she'd even be in North Bergen, for that matter. But before any harm was actually done, she presented each with a signed photo of herself. Typical Bette.

I'll never forget the night Bette Davis became a car hiker. The car parkers for the restaurant wore red wool coats with gold braiding and red stocking caps. And they carried flashlights. "Now *that* would be a fun job!" she announced, marching off toward the drop off spot on the Chateau's long circular driveway. In seconds, she persuaded one of the car hikers to lend her his coat, cap and flash-

This place looked like Las Vegas met the "Merchant of Venice."

light. The big pair of sunglasses was her own addition to the ensemble. The next thing I knew she was waving the flashlight around, directing traffic through the entrance and yelling "*Pahk right here! Pahk right here!*"

None of the patrons knew that it was Bette Davis guiding them in. Who'd even suspect? To this day, I wonder how they would have reacted if they had. Would they have stopped and stared? And what if she'd actually taken the keys and parked their cars for them? Would they have given her a tip? And how much is the proper tip for *Bette Davis: Car Hiker*? Miss Manners never covered that!

She was having a ball, and actually doing a pretty good job. But after about fifteen minutes she got bored with the whole exercise. "I *turned* in my coat," she announced. "*Not* a good ca-reer move either," she added, and then she started laughing. "Think what the *pa*-pers would say! '*Now Bette Davis Is Parking Cars For A Living!*'"

Not too long after that my agent called with the best news I could have ever heard! The Hotels

Ambassador had been sold to the Loew's Hotels. They planned a major renovation. And the new owners wanted me to come back to The Pump Room! Preston Robert Tisch and his brother, Lawrence, were offering a one year contract, with an option to renew. Was I interested? Interested? I was ecstatic!

I would open again at the Pump Room on the 26th of October, 1965, about eight months after I'd left. When the plane set down at O'Hare again on that early Sunday afternoon, I was back, but different. I was confident. And the one-year contract in my inside coat pocket certainly helped!

"Welcome back, Mr. Paul," the doorman smiled and shook my hand when I stepped out of the taxi. When I walked into the hotel, I had to smile as I approached the front desk and saw myself immortalized again on a sign that stood on the very same easel.

> **Stanley Paul**
> **and**
> **His East Coast Society Orchestra**
> **Opening in the Pump Room**
> **Tuesday Night**

My first thought was, "There they go with the East Coast bit again," but it was good to be back. I liked the feeling, and before I did anything else, I hurried up the three carpeted stairs to the Pump Room. I took a deep breath and walked through the door. All the captains and waiters came over to shake my hand and welcome me back. The moment the maitre d' laid eyes on me, he pointed to an open booth, ordered me to have dinner on the house and muttered that I was "still a skinny runt." I was home.

David Mall and his orchestra played the room on Sunday and Monday evenings, my days off. On my way up to the bandstand to say hello, I was stopped by the Kupcinets, in Booth One of course. They welcomed me back, then they invited me to join them "out on the town" the next evening. I couldn't wait to get filled in from "the source" themselves on all that I'd missed in my eight month absence. They'd come to the Pump Room just about every evening of my stay there the previous year, but at this point, we still hadn't been out socially together. This was quite an invitation and I was excited.

The next evening I met them at their apartment around half past five. After we watched the news on TV, we began the evening with dinner at Fritzel's, which was one of the "in" places in Chicago at the time. Later, that location became a men's clothing store and now it is the home to several fast-food restaurants, but once it was the place to have a lunch or early dinner.

Then we were off to the Conrad Hilton for a political reception where I met several people I'd only read about up to that point. I was introduced to the Mayor and Mrs. Richard J. Daley. What a welcome back night this was turning out to be—and it had only begun!

After about an hour hobnobbing with the most powerful politicians in Chicago and the state, we went across the hall to see the Ice Show in the Boulevard Room of the Hilton. At the time, that hotel featured a full skating extravaganza, with long-legged women gliding through figure eights and clowns who could skate over barrels as a full orchestra accompanied them.

Then it was time for another taxi ride a few blocks north to the Empire Room at the Palmer House to catch Jimmy Durante's show in which he pounded the piano, cracked jokes in his Brooklyn accent and sang his signature "Inka Dinka Do."

The wonderful Jimmy Durante.

Next, it was up to Rush Street to hear Totie Fields breaking up the audience at Mr. Kelly's, the nightclub which always booked the funniest comedians and best singers.

Of course, being with *Mr. and Mrs. Chicago* meant a ringside table wherever we went. It also guaranteed perfect service. I was impressed!

It was a typical whirlwind evening for Irv and Essee, but unheard of for this so-called society band leader from New York.

By 2 a.m., I was completely exhausted, but the Kups were still going strong. Actually, they seemed to get more energy the later it got, as Essee cracked jokes about Irv's penchant for napping during dull theatrical performances and Irv smiled and enjoyed every minute. When we stopped at The Singapore on Rush Street for perfectly cooked ribs, I all but fell asleep at the table.

Early the next morning, as I was still collapsed in bed, I watched Kup live on my television screen, reporting on the Chicago scene and looking perfectly fresh and alert. I don't know how they did that, but they did it *every night*!

The next night I opened to a packed house. It seemed like everyone I had met in Chicago was there along with representatives of all the newspapers. As I made my way up to the bandstand, I was completely energized. Getting up on that bandstand that night was like riding a bicycle after a long absence—everything came back to me. The place was *jumpin'* in minutes and I'd never been more comfortable in my life. It was wonderful!

"Cocktails, dinner, music, dancing, hugs and kisses and talk and talk and talk!

(Chicago Historical Society photo)

The original Mr. Kellys, now the home of Gibsons Steakhouse, a popular Chicago watering hole.

They practiced the art, or maybe we should say, the craft of conversation with a controlled abandon." I never was able to identify who wrote this about the Pump Room, but I never forgot it. It's what the room was really like! And that's the way it was that night—as always.

Announcing my return to the Pump Room. Note that my local musicians are still an "East Coast Society Orchestra."

Three more nights of warm greetings and glowing reviews, and then Saturday, the hottest night of the week, arrived. It was *always* the hottest. People stayed out late, dressed to the hilt, partied hard and wanted to be seen! And the jewels! I'd never seen so many women wearing such expensive jewelry. It was a time when no one seemed concerned about the safety factor.

And the latest fashions! Hemlines were dramatically changing in those days, moving up or down with every hiccup of the stock market. If John

Fairchild of Women's Wear Daily decreed the newest skirt length was the mini or maxi, whispering to the knee or just south of your mother's worst nightmare, you can bet that's the length I'd be seeing in the room the following Saturday night.

Fashion could also cause problems. There was a time when all the younger women put thick falls in their hair. One night, a woman's fall was actually speared by one of the waiters' flaming swords! It smelled awful, but then I suppose the room was lucky her hair spray didn't ignite!

"We'd planned all week what we'd wear to the Pump Room on Saturday night!" said Carol Ware, who, with her husband Irwin, ran their fabulous fur salons in Chicago in those years. She remembered a lady who spent almost every week in Florida, perfecting her tan so she could return to Chicago and wow every one in the Pump Room on Saturday night.

The booths would start filling about 6:30 p.m., and the maitre d' would be answering two phones at a time, confirming reservations and the booth in which each party would be seated. The big power play was to get a booth or a table near Booth One,

Saturday night at the Pump Room.

so you could be seen as well as have a bird's eye view of the VIPs. Tourists, or customers other than regulars would often be seated on the balcony, near the band, or near the kitchen in places that were Pump Room versions of Siberia. It wasn't required to have a triple A Standard & Poor's rating, or income in the seven figures, or a hit record, book, TV show or movie to sit in or near Booth One, but those sorts of things helped guarantee the better seating.

I would get to the room about 7:30 and start our first dance set at 8 p.m. Before I ever got to the bandstand, it'd be like old home week as I made my way around the floor greeting patrons. I got to know most of them. By the time we began our first set, the room would be completely full. It would stay that way until closing.

We played the rhythms of the day—Bossa Novas, Cha Chas, and lots of two-beat swing music. We never played rock 'n roll, which wasn't exactly outlawed in the Pump Room. It was merely frowned upon because patrons couldn't two-step, box-step or waltz to rock's rhythms. I enjoyed playing Meringues and Rhumbas, because it was so much fun to watch the attitudes people assumed when they did those dances.

The second shift of patrons would start arriving around 9:30 or ten. Sometimes they joined others already at tables and booths, and seating for four would swell to eight, with extra chairs appearing everywhere. The captains and waiters were busy rolling carts down the aisles, making Caesar salads and serving steak tartar at the tables, or lighting flaming dishes. Others would serve crab meat wrapped in bacon or shish-que-bob.

People would be paged at their booths with telephones brought to them and plugged into jacks. Getting a call on a Saturday night at the Pump Room was the height of importance—no one would interrupt the boss on a Saturday night for anything but an emergency or intense romantic difficulties. There were cigarette packs open at every table—remember this was a time when almost everyone smoked, even doctors. The patrons inhabited a blue haze of sophistication and no one ever said the word 'carcinogens.' Other people stood in line, waiting for customers to finish and vacate their booths, but people always seemed to linger at their tables. No one wanted to leave when the room was just hitting its stride!

By eleven, the lobby was usually filled with patrons trying to get into the Pump Room, tips passing frantically to the maitre d' or anyone with an inside track on a table. Inside, people were standing four deep at the bar, talking to each other while trying to be not too obvious when they tried to figure out if a celebrity was really sitting in Booth One. Scotch, bourbon, manhattans and martinis were the drinks of choice.

The maitre d' would be beside himself by now, but invisibly so. He never showed it, but once you got to know him you could tell when his nerves began to strain. Just around midnight like clockwork, a hush would come over the room. I didn't even have to look at the door. I knew who it was who'd arrived. Why it was May Darling, of course!

Who was May Darling? When people talk about the Pump Room in the 1960s, the first thing they usually ask me is "Do you remember that old lady with the flashlights?" Do I! No recollection of the place would be complete without her.

"Princess of the Pump Room."

Once dubbed Princess of the Pump Room, May Darling started coming there when she was in her late seventies, and continued until her death at the age of eighty-eight. One of those sights you had to see to believe—long platinum blonde wigs that looked like hand-me-downs from retired streetwalkers, makeup by Earl Scheib Paint & Body and enough ostrich feathers to denude an entire flock! She looked like she had kidnapped a continent's worth of ostriches, dyed each bird a different color and then draped them all around her neck at the same time.

She made all of her own gowns, and they were intensely original creations she'd dream up under the influence of indigestion. While her costumes were an unspoken challenge to the grande lady of camp herself, Mae West, certainly no dress designer in his or her right mind would ever want to take credit for her bizarre, individualistic results, which were heavy with spangles, sequins, fake emeralds and pearls nestled into heavily draped bodices and on long, flowing skirts suitable for a duchess attending a minor coronation.

Miss Darling and her beau, George Wriberg, carried everything she wore (or twirled) to the Pump Room and back home again every week, and there was a lot to carry! They lived way up on the north side of the city, far from the denizens of Booth One. They would commute to the Pump Room by bus, alighting at the stop about a block from the hotel and walking the rest of the way. The sight of them shlepping hat boxes from Mandel Brothers, which had been closed for years, and various and sundry costume items down the street was a sight in itself.

They came in the Ambassador West entrance, and Miss Darling would change into her creations in the ladies room there. George would drape all her paste jewelry around her neck while they stood in the lobby, making sure there were enough Woolworth's "diamond" bracelets to cover both arms. How she was able to get her arms up to put those flashlights in place, I'll never know, but then, I'm coming to that.

Anyway, when she was completely outfitted, the two of them marched along Milsom Street (the arcade through the tunnel that connects the Ambassador West and Ambassador East hotels) went up the elevator to the lobby and into the Pump Room.

Her not-so-royal-highness May Darling, and her Prince Consort would strut down the aisle to their usual table—the one next to the trumpet player. It was the loudest table in the house, but it was on the balcony adjoining the bandstand, where she had a full view of the room. She loved it. She also loved the fact that everyone in the room had a full view of May.

Once seated, this extremely odd couple's order was always the same, one chicken sandwich, which they'd split and enjoy throughout the evening, and two bourbons, which they also nursed all night long. Because they were a most memorable couple and because they were beloved, throughout the evening waiters would give them French pastry while many customers would send over champagne.

Miss Darling always brought her photographs with her and they would be spread out at her table, ready to be autographed for anyone who asked. She offered a dozen different poses of herself and some of the views of May dating back nearly to the turn of the century when she claimed she'd studied with Flo Ziegfield's father. She loved to tell everyone and anyone that she had been in the Ziegfield Follies. Whether it was true or not didn't really matter. No one was around who could or would dispute the story. What was important was that talking about the legends of Miss Darling seemed to make May happy. And it was fun to hear her tell them.

The May and George "show" would start when we'd strike up *Hello Dolly,* which was May's signal to go out on the dance floor. She'd glance at us and we'd all yell "You're on May!" George would stand up and pull her chair out for her, then she'd check her make-up, adjust the flash-lights in her bosom so they would be providing spotlights for her face, and the two of them would walk grandly towards the dance floor.

Needless to say, the floor cleared and people made a circle around as she did her bumps and grinds with a flashlight shining down each bosom and two more that George had focused on her from different angles. Come to think of it, May Darling probably created the first "sound and light show," but credit for that has been denied her!

The "May and George Show."

George acted like a bodyguard, keeping people from getting very close. I think he really believed that every man was out to steal her from him.

George was at his most jealous one evening when Frank Sinatra was sitting in Booth One with his friend, Jilly Rizzo, a big guy who could be tough when the occasion demanded. May was so excited about Sinatra being there that she kept walking back and forth in front of his booth. But that wasn't all. She was winking at him! She even stopped and dropped a handkerchief to get his attention. She was, I must admit, being shameless, especially for a woman well into her seventh decade.

Frank was doubled over with laughter. Every time he looked up, she'd be strutting in front of him with her hands on her hips looking like a French tart who lost a lamp post to lean against. He'd just stare for a moment, put down his head and lose it. He was actually hysterical, with tears rolling down his face, laughing so hard he found it difficult to breathe. And every time she'd walk by and give him a wink, he'd lose it again!

George, who was fuming at this point, was ready to lose it himself. He marched up to the bandstand and said to me, "If that *crooner* doesn't stop flirting with my little girl, I'm going to bop him one!"

I'm thinking "*My little girl?!*" Sure, when State Street was a prairie!

When I introduced May to Judy Garland, May kept telling Judy how much she enjoyed one of her recent pictures. "Dear, I don't remember the title, but it was the one where you sang that song about the trolley." she said, describing *Meet Me in Saint Louis.* May repeatedly predicted, "Dear, you have a *great* future!" Their conversation took place in 1967. Unfortunately, the film had been released in 1944!

In the late 1960s, May had her costume break-through when the warehouse that stored all Sonja Henie's costumes from the Ice Reviews had a close-out sale. She was elated! May and George were there from morning until night. She bought and bought and bought, coming away with all sorts of unusual items, including several enormous headpieces that required chin straps! All these treasures were purchased for next to nothing because who else would wear them? One of the headpieces proved to be so tall and elaborately adorned that she had trouble getting through the door to the Pump Room one Saturday night because its feathers kept getting caught in the chandeliers. We were lucky there were no ceiling fans or May's head might have been unscrewed.

How could Frank Sinatra resist May Darling?

One Saturday evening I was sitting with Edith Head, the famous Hollywood costume designer, and I started to talk about the character who'd soon be arriving. I described May, as best as I could, but Edith just kept peering at me through those tinted eyeglasses she wore. "Stanley, I *do* love your stories, you've such a vivid imagination."

Imagination! I knew that May would be getting ready for her entrance because it was something you could almost set your watch by, so I excused myself and headed for the lobby. She was putting her flashlights in place before her grand entrance. I told her, "Edith Head is here. You know the costume designer who wins all the Oscars. You'll really want to meet her!"

As I entered the room with May, George was following close behind, watching my every move. I escorted her to Booth One and May cried, loud enough for even this noisy room to hear, "Oh Miss Head! I get *all* my inspiration for my designs from *you*!"

Edith simply nodded her head and smiled, slumping progressively lower in her seat as though she'd like to disappear into the floor. As George was escorting May to their table, Edith followed

them all the way there with her eyes, sighed and said "It's time for me to retire."

By one in the morning the room was always still crowded. It didn't seem to matter where you'd been to dinner or what shows you'd seen, you couldn't end a Saturday evening in Chicago anywhere else but the Pump Room, at the Ambassador East. I think it was as much a state of mind as it was the actual place.

Weeks passed quickly, it seemed, and it wasn't too long after my return that the Tisch brothers finally announced that they'd hired Richard Himmel, a well known Chicago designer, to give the hotel and its famous Pump Room its multimillion dollar face lift. Their intention was to restore the room's grandeur, and it was estimated that the project would take several weeks. For months people spoke of little else, curious as to the changes they had in mind. When the Pump Room closed that summer, everyone waited with baited breath for its doors to open again.

Six weeks later, on the night of September 8th, 1966, the Pump Room had its Grand Reopening Celebration, and the new room was a sight to behold! It was still a glimmering castle, with great crystal chandeliers. Wagons, waiters, bus boys and flaming swords were still in a constant state of motion, and the buzz of conversation rose and fell with the same gentle constancy. But now, there was a new depth, a new richness about the place. The walls were hung with a deep blue fabric and even the darks were darker. There was a magic to the remodeling, which offered an attention to detail that hadn't been there before while keeping the same feelings of grandeur and importance. The renovation was no less than a masterpiece!

My piano was still in the far left corner of the room, but it was white now, just as I'd requested! The larger stage I'd also asked for was significantly bigger.

But as striking as the improvements made to the room's physical features had been, the addition of two individuals in particular to the staff was more than masterful. That was a stroke of genius!

Monsieur Victor Jabeneau.

The first of these was a new face greeting patrons at the entrance Monsieur Victor Jabeneau, *maitre d' extraordinaire.* He stood, facing out, at the waist-high reservation desk just inside the entrance, making a magnificent appearance in white tie and tails. Tall, with a perfectly straight posture that made him seem even taller, he was a man with an air of warmth and grace. When he stood at the door, the great leather reservations book of inscribed names, dates and times was always open before him.

"Good evening, Mr. and Mrs. so and so . . ." would roll gently from his tongue in a deep French accent. He'd often bow at the waist before a woman with whom he was acquainted, then gently take her hand in his and kiss it. He was the embodiment of continental elegance exactly as the original vision of creator of the Pump Room, Ernie Byfield, would have dictated.

Over the years, the ever-suave Victor was strained by the changes in fashion. He almost went berserk when he had to let Sonny Bono in to the Pump Room without a tie, breaking a rule that had been firmly enforced since the day the room opened. A few days later, Victor was inwardly apoplectic when Barbra Streisand breezed through the door in a too tight pants suit. Outwardly, he was as gracious as ever.

The second addition was the consummate public relations person, Lucia Perrigo, who had finally returned to The Pump Room after spending a few years promoting Maxim's, the French restaurant in the lower level of the Astor Towers, which was only a half block east of the Ambassador. Lucia was back, out classing, out talking and out energizing everyone in the business. Lucia seemed to do everything all at once. I remember seeing her talk on four phones at the same time while writing a press release and being interviewed by reporters. She could make things happen and, for every minute of every year she stayed there with us, she did.

On the night of the Pump Room's Grand Re-Opening Celebration, she'd reinitiated the custom of bringing stars from the Ambassador West to the Ambassador East in the sedan chair. Ray Bolger, the dancer in so many film musicals, made his entrance hoisted by four elegantly costumed carriers. That night, it seemed as though the 18th century took over most of the room!

Lucia Perrigo with "Tell it to Louella" Parsons. Samuel Goldwyn once quipped "Louella Parsons is stronger than Samson. He needed two columns to bring the house down, Louella could do it with one!"

(Townsfolk Magazine)

"Boy, did that powderd wig itch!"

It was a star studded evening at the Beau Nasn Revel when the splendid new Pump Room of the Ambassador East Hotel was un-veiled at a black tie benefit sponsored by the North Avenue Day Nursery, the same charity which heralded the Pump Room when it made its debut in 1938. Among gay celebrants toasting a portrait of Beau Nash, Master of Ceremonies of the original Pump Room 200 years ago, were Mrs. Ward Nixon, Mrs. James Magin, and Stanley Paul.

Peter Duchin, my New York buddy stopped by and congratulates me on my new one year contract.

Thanks to Lucia, the re-opening received considerable advance press. Herb Lyon described the plans in his Tower Ticker column that morning:

> "The Ambassador's famed Pump Room, its face lifted and glowing, reopens tonight with hoo-hoo-hoopla (via a black-tie benefit for the North Avenue Day Nursery), 'Mongst the whoop-it uppers: Jack Benny; Ray Bolger and Kukla, Fran and Ollie (that's Burr Tillstrom and Fran Allison); Admr. Howard Yeager (commandant of Great Lakes); Eve ("Hello Dolly") Arden and her hubby, Brooks West; Joan (Ivanhoe) Claufield. Plus the beaming Ambassador bosses, Bob and Larry Tisch. P.S. Suave Pump Room maestro Stan Paul has composed a snappy, special score, "The Belles of the Bath" and "Beau Nash Revel."

All in all, everything was wonderful! As was the next evening, and every one that followed. I was happier than I'd ever been and settling in!

As part of the 1966 restoration, I'd been given a new suite on the sixth floor that was much bigger than the one I'd had before. My first thought was, "My piano finally has some room around it!" until I considered furniture, of which, I had none!

And I had no budget for furniture, especially the sorts of pieces which would fit in a hotel like the Ambassador, so I started scouring the thrift shops and antique shops on Clark Street. "Bonnie and Clyde" had just been released and I loved their '30s look. The Kupcinets had introduced me to a new friend, Burr Tillstrom, of *Kukla, Fran and Ollie* fame and he had a station wagon! He was nice enough to drive me around to these shops and haul my purchases back to the hotel for me. He laughed a lot. His most repeated phrase was, "You're nuts to buy this junk!"

Everything I purchased was, or would soon be, black, white or silver. I liked the look of it. It had a style that appealed to the heart of me and still does.

It was used furniture though and it needed some work. Luckily, the Hotels Ambassador provided me with quite a few resources. They had a carpentry shop where, for just a few bucks, I could get anything that I needed refinished. I only wish I could still get that deal today. There was a hotel upholstery shop where I'd bring over-stuffed furniture and some inexpensive fabrics to be transformed into exactly what I wanted.

The resource that would prove most valuable, however, was in the basement! It was a storage area where paintings and antiques were stored, to be brought to the VIP suites for special guests on an "as needed" basis. Within days, my suite became the hotels' new storage facility! If anything was ever missing from the basement storage area, everyone in the hotel knew where it could most likely be found. I would often return to find great spaces on my walls where paintings had been needed, located and removed. Call it my revolving art collection, but that was okay by me. I was flexible.

By the time I finished, the apartment was not only different for its time, it was stunning, and I don't think I spent more than about $700 for all the furniture! Before long, my suite started getting a lot of press. "Art Deco," they called it. As it became an attraction of the house, so to speak, people started asking to see it!

"I would have loved to live in the '30's." Swing bandleader Stanley Paul is making his wish come true—at least in his apartment.

Chicago's American photos
by Carl Hugare

The musician created a gray and green marble effect on his hallway walls to obtain a stucco effect. Glassless, black and white prints of the Paranaise cover one wall over a thin box of plastic fronds and ivy under the shadowing, branch-wrapped light fixture.

The living room almost breathes '30s atmosphere. Heavily fringed matte silk drapery hangs over a wall of window sheets. A plush, crushed velvet couch in matching beige stands near potted palms spreading from the room's corners.

Sheet music from the period and ivy cover his vintage piano and accessories in every corner of the room carry out the decor.

A silver butter dish on a Sheffield tray rests on one table, silver cigaret box and decanters on another. A silver desk set and a chandelier table lamp glitter and reflect images in a wall arrangement of mirror and glass-framed pictures nearby.

Chicago's American, Sunday, Dec 10, 1967

Apartment recaptures the '30s mood

Bonnie and Clyde were born too early. Or Stanley Paul was born too late.

Either way, the Pump room band leader who specializes in the 1930 swing sound has found a way to recreate the era in his apartment by reclaiming furniture from the hotel storeroom.

"Most of it was put away a long time ago, and some of it was still in good condition.

A door in one corner opens to a closet-sized kitchen which Paul has hung with song sheets from 1910 to 1930. Curlicue designs cover the vintage appliances and tiffany trims the light fixture.

But it's the bedroom which is the most dramatic presentation. Modern 1930 black with silver chests and matching felt bed headboard offset a black leather bedspread over an underskirting of soft green fabric.

A silver painted molding saved from the ruins of the Plaza hotel frames a bigger-than-life photo of film star Jean Harlow over the bed. Silver sprayed reliefs saved from old theaters shine from the wall.

A 1930 radio coated in aluminum paint looks down at a sun chair which once decked the hotel roof during the same decade.

Modern glass and wood block based lamps with squared shades pick up the line of a lacquered black cabinet with zebra skin front which houses a stereo and collection of Rudy Vallee records.

A silver, white, and ebony balloon chandelier dangles from the ceiling, contrasting, the height of a towering white column at the door footed with psychedelic print pillows. Ebony drapes finish the decor with hanging felt cornice and check design.

Authentics are everywhere. A Duke of Windsor lighter molded to a polo pony and player image stands on a bureau. Not far away is one of the first pictures of Bette Davis after she arrived in Hollywood. The photo was a gift from the star to Paul.

"I love that era," said Paul. "I wish I had lived in it—this is the closest I came to it."

Polly Sheridan

"Even Bette sent me her first Hollywood photo taken in 1931 for my piano."

My boss Preston Robert Tisch shows Robert Kennedy the new remodeled Pump Room—1966.

Ginger Rogers at lunch one afternoon.

Kup with Lee Bouvier Radziwell. The local papers were agog that Jackie Kennedy's sister was going to make her acting debut in Chicago. Lee Bouvier, who was known as Princess Radziwill since her marriage to someone with a title, was going to appear at the Ivanhoe Theater in "The Philadelphia Story." I was there for Miss Bouvier's opening night. Prince Stanislaw (Stash) Radziwill, her husband, was there puffing on a cigarette in a holder and constantly answering the question, ""How's she doin', Prince?" It seemed like half the world's press were there to watch her debut. Having seen that moment in theater history, the safest thing to say was that she knew her lines.

From left to right: Milton Berle, Irv Kupcinet, Essee Kupcinet, person unknown, Marshall Korshak, Jake Arvey-Standing, Ray Bolger, Wes Addy, Celeste Holm. Beau Nash Club 2nd Floor 1966.

With Zsa Zsa Gabor. She was absolutely gorgeous, spoiled rotten—always the ultimate movie star— only now I can't remember one damn movie she ever made!

Tony Bennett has Barbara Rush's attention serenading at a Sarah Siddons Award.

Mrs. Loyal Davis with Brittish musical comedy star Tommy Steele. Edie Davis, who was Nancy Reagan's mother, was known for her risque stories. I remember, she was telling a group of people an off color joke as I approached her booth—she stopped mid sentence— "Stanley, you are too young to hear this!"

Is Jane Russell telling Bob Hope "Thanks for the memories?"

The afternoon Gypsy Rose Lee was the guest star at luncheon fashion show. Gypsy decided to spice it up a little, the problem was, she hadn't worn that costume in a few years and they had a little trouble getting her zipped up. The end result, she had as much cleavage in the back as the front!

Two grande dames; Celeste Holm and Helen Hayes.

Ronald Reagan showing new family photos to his mother-in-law, Mrs. Loyal Davis.

I played for dinner on Wednesday through Sunday evenings, beginning at 7:30, and made it a point to be able to play something personal for special guests who visited the room. I'd developed a system with Victor, who'd give me a cue as the celebrities began their ascent up the three stairs that led to the entrance. By the time they passed through the doorway, I'd be playing a recognizable melody. It was a salute to them, the personal touch that said hello. It established rapport. I was the musical ambassador of the Ambassador, and I loved every moment of it!

On any given night I was in my tuxedo playing Cole Porter and Gershwin, waiting for the cue from Victor to stop the band and play *Thanks for the Memories* for Bob Hope, *Hello Dolly* or *Diamonds Are a Girl's Best Friend* for Carol Channing or *Somewhere Over the Rainbow* for Judy Garland. George Jessel almost fainted on the dance floor when I played *Baby Blue Eyes* for him. He'd written the song forty-six years before, for a show called *Troubles of 1922.*

Henny Youngman once walked in three times before Victor was able to catch my eye, the signal to play his song, *Smoke Gets in Your Eyes.* Maybe on that night both smoke and stars were in my eyes.

Ann Miller and her hair were frequent guests at the fashion shows.

A hug from Arlene Francis.

CHAPTER EIGHT

STAR TIME

For the next several years, just about any star in town promoting a movie or a book, or appearing in a local production at the Drury Lane, Ivanhoe or Shubert Theaters and several other regional theatres would either be staying at the hotel or just coming to the Pump Room.

What a thrill it was to meet and play for Ethel Waters.

We put a candleabra on the piano to honor Liberace for this photo shoot.

I thought "What the hell am I supposed to call him? Mr. Tim?, Mr. Tiny?"

Burr Tillstrom taking to the floor with the lovely Ann Baxter.

Donna Beaumont Atwater takes a whirl with Henry Fonda.

With Pearl Bailey; Pearl was a nightly visitor in booth one during her lengthy run in "Hello Dolly" 1971.

The celebrities who hung out there had often just finished their own shows a few hours before. Lonely, tired of being on the road, or just needing someone to talk with, they would gravitate to Booth One, where we would meet and usually discover something we had in common. It might be that we shared friends in the roving gypsy community of performers, or that we were night people, or that we had similar interests in music or theater. Or it might just be that I was a good listener. Whatever the reason, for someone as star struck as I was, a 'kid in a candy store' is one cliché that fit perfectly.

Three weeks before Phyllis Dillers first face lift. She came back 8 weeks later looking absolutely gorgeous—well, maybe pretty.

After the Pump Room closed for the night at 1:15 or so, many visiting celebrities were invited upstairs to my suite as a matter of course. It often became a private party night. The kitchen occasionally sent up caviar and champagne in great gleaming buckets.

Pearl with husband Louis Bellson at a party in my apartment.

With my old New York pal Eileen Brennan before her stardom in "Private Benjamin."

Carol Channing hams it up at my piano.

The next morning Herb Lyon, Jon and Abra, Maggie Daly or Bob Weidrich, local columnists who might have called the night before, would have items about who'd been at my apartment the previous night. Irv Kupcinet of the Chicago Sun-Times never called, though. Somehow, he already knew! I remember when Jane Russell, once the reigning sex symbol, was in my living room when there was this call about 1:30 in the morning. It was Kup and his first words to me were, "Stanley, lemme talk to Jane." Well, that's Kup!

Many a night these stars would talk and talk until the wee hours, and in that time I heard some funny, fascinating stories. And I also heard some personal, even intimate ones told in confidence. I respected that then and will continue to do so to this day. Since many of the people who stayed up all night with me are no longer living, they cannot defend themselves. But the promises I made when they were alive still apply.

I'm disturbed by books that reveal intimate details that were never meant to be broadcast. We're living in a time when almost everyone tells too much and its creating a sadder, meaner representation of what was actually a dazzling, glamorous era.

These stories hold memories of cherished moments for me. Each of them are tales the stars either told on themselves in public or were ones that my friends have encouraged me to reveal.

GLORIA SWANSON

NEVER CASUAL

When people think of Gloria Swanson, I think the Norma Desmond character from Sunset Boulevard comes to mind. She was the somewhat demented, has-been Hollywood movie star, living in self imposed isolation, answering fan mail written by her also somewhat crazed but devoted butler, and ordering people to do things for her as though she were the Queen of Sheba! It turned out to be the

With Gloria Swanson.

role for which she was most famous, but her actual personality was nothing like that at all, though she did have several queen-like characteristics.

For instance, there was the first time I met her. She arrived at my suite to discuss the musical arrangements I'd be playing for a new show she was going to do in Chicago called *Reprise,* opening at the Ivanhoe Theater. She was strikingly attractive. A tiny woman, wearing very little make-up with beautiful skin that looked remarkably ageless even though she was in her 70s. And she was sporting a very chic suit with a mini-skirt and black kid knee high boots! I don't know what it was I'd expected, but it wasn't that. Nothing about her was very much like what I might have expected, I'd soon discover.

She made herself comfortable in the living room while I went to the kitchen to get some refreshments, and when I came back a few minutes later, I was surprised to see Miss Swanson moving furniture around and setting up the scene! As I stood in the doorway staring at her, she picked the piano bench up into her arms and carried it off to the hallway!

My sudden thought was, "And what am I supposed to sit on?"

Soon the entire place was rearranged and I was left to stand, *sans* bench, at my piano. I scribbled the music onto a page and then hunched over the piano Jerry Lee Lewis style, while she pranced around the room saying things like "I will walk to *this* position and will need about 20 seconds of background music." Then she'd stop, look at me, make a few gestures and march off to another corner, move more chairs out of the way and say "Then I'll move over *here.* You'll need to play while I'm walking, but stop when I do *this . . .*" With that she turned, raised one arm and pretended to be speaking.

On and on she went, moving through one scene after another like a tornado. All the music was written after about an hour or so, but my back

didn't recover for another two weeks! I never took my piano bench for granted again after that.

We spent a great deal of time together during her stay here, and she told me that she was one of the first stars to sing in a talkie movie. And then she played me a recording of the song she'd done for her sound debut, *Love, Your Magic Spell Is Everywhere,* from the 1929 movie *Trespasser.* I asked her to sing while I played for her, and I was surprised to discover that she had a finely trained operatic voice. Not *great,* but not bad either!

"Ever think about doing an album?" I asked. We discussed it, and she thought it might be worth a try, then we made a date to get together for an informal rehearsal a few days later. She arrived right on time and we got down to business immediately, as was her style. The rehearsal was going remarkably well. We were rolling along nicely through one number after another until I ruined it all by opening my big mouth.

"Gloria, I just had an idea for the cover of the album!" I blurted out, moved by some sudden inspiration. "You could be photographed in *color,* and the background could be all black and whites. They could use all those wonderful stills from your days in Hollywood!"

That was all I had to say. She said nothing at first, then her eyes widened and her face just started glowing! "I could wear red!" she said. Then, rising to her feet, stretching her arms out to her sides, and assuming different positions in the room, in front of each of several movie stills she kept envisioning. "Imagine *this!*" she kept saying.

From that point on all she was interested in is what she would wear for that damned cover! What it would look like. Which pictures we'd use. Whether we ought to take new ones. She became bored with the musical part entirely, and we never had another rehearsal. And then, just as quickly as the album idea had come to mind . . . it quietly disappeared.

Several days later, some of the members of her show were having a cast party and she asked me if I'd accompany her. It was on one of my nights off at the Pump Room, so I gladly agreed. The party was being held in a fourth floor walk-up apartment. Since she was at least seventy years old, all the way there I was worrying about what I'd do if she couldn't make it up the stairs. Could I catch her if something happened? But as things turned out, I was the one that had trouble catching my breath. She bounded past me, two stairs at a time, and then stood up there on the landing waiting.

While I huffed and puffed my way up after her she kept preaching at me!

"It's those damn cigarettes, Stanley," she scolded. "I told you, you aren't eating properly. You eat all that horrible junk food!" Junk food was a relatively new term then, but Gloria was one of the first health food enthusiasts.

From that night on, she was on a mission to change my eating habits. "Just chew on these," she instructed one afternoon, while stuffing some egg shells into my mouth. "It'll put potassium in your diet. It's good for you!"

Well, of course I chewed on them. And of course I swallowed them too, as she insisted. I even tried the carrot juice she presented, instantly manufactured before my eyes! The woman actually traveled with her own vegetable juicer in her luggage! I kept asking myself, who would ever think of doing something like that?

The next afternoon was very hot and very sunny. I was lying by the water at the Oak Street Beach when I suddenly doubled up in pain. It was excruciating! My friends just watched me going through all these gyrations for awhile, then hauled me off to the closest hospital. There X-rays revealed that egg shells had lodged in my stomach lining! "So much for healthy living . . ." I thought, and lit up another cigarette.

The most typical Gloria Swanson adventure happened when she called me one afternoon and said she wanted to go to that place "where all the cast members go."

"You mean Punchinello's?" I answered.

"Yes!" she exclaimed. "That sounds like it. It's a night club isn't it? How shall I dress?"

I tried to explain that it wasn't so much a night club as just a casual sort of place on Rush Street. Show business types appearing in all sorts of shows all over the city would go there after their performances.

"They dress really casual," I said. "Shirts and blue jeans sort of thing. I'm not sure you'd be very comfortable at all." Personally, I doubt the word casual had ever been included in Gloria Swanson's vocabulary, but everyone went there, and she didn't want to be left out. So, casual or not, we were going!

The next night Victor sent a note up to the bandstand at about one o'clock in the morning that said Miss Swanson was waiting. It was late, and the room was nearly empty, so I cut the set short and ducked out a little early. When I got to the lobby, there she was, every inch the movie star, wearing a huge hat, gloves, diamonds and dripping in sables.

"Casual . . ." I thought to myself, smiling. She's ready to make a grand entrance at Ciro's, circa 1940! I'd planned to run upstairs and change into a sweater and slacks, but when confronted with this vision, I really had no choice but to stay dressed in my tuxedo.

"Stanley, when we get there let's just stay in the back," she was saying in the cab. "I don't want to cause a *fuss* or anything. We'll just blend in with everyone else."

What did the Madam who wished to "just blend in" do? She walked straight through the entrance to a table right near the piano, directly beneath the spotlight, as if drawn to the one place in the room that was exactly center stage. With every eye in the place riveted on her, she raised her gloved hand and said, "Waiter . . . we will both have mineral water!"

Then she turned to me and said, "They're staring Stanley, do you believe it? I don't know how they always find me. They do though . . . don't they!"

Several years later she was back in Chicago as the featured guest at the Book Sellers' Convention Banquet. She'd just completed her autobiography, *Swanson On Swanson*, and was in the middle of a cross-country tour promoting the book. I was handling the music for the event at the Marriott Hotel on Michigan Avenue

We stood together in the lobby a few minutes before she was about to make her entrance. She was so much older looking now, and so frail, but with a slight twinkle in those tired eyes. Then Merv Griffin took the mike and announced "And here she is! The woman who invented Hollywood

Gloria in town to promote "Swanson on Swanson."

. . . the legendary . . . Miss Gloria ***Swanson!***"

We struck up her song, *Love, Your Magic Spell Is Everywhere,* hardly discernible over the nearly deafening applause and the most extraordinary thing happened! The older, frail, tired looking woman I'd met in the lobby had completely transformed herself. She was standing in her spotlight, just as she'd done

that night in Punchinello's. She floated across the dance floor to the stage, literally prancing through the audience and flashing that famous Gloria Swanson smile. Ageless still. The embodiment of grace. It was the way I will always remember her.

ETHEL MERMAN

THE VOICE

I'll never forget the first evening Ethel Merman came to the Pump Room when I was leading the orchestra. No matter what anyone thought of Merman's voice, this lady had introduced more Broadway hits than anyone. George Gershwin wrote her first show in 1930 called *Girl Crazy* and that made her a star. "Don't ever take singing lessons Ethel, you'll ruin your voice!" he'd advised her. Cole Porter, who wrote four shows for her, said she sounded like a brass band, and Irving Berlin loved to write for her. They loved to use her because in the '30s and '40s, before they used microphones in Broadway shows, her voice could fill the theater. So her voice certainly filled the entire room that night.

Because I'm a big fan of Broadway musicals, I'd learned most of the songs that made her famous. For over an hour that evening I played a Merman Marathon. Then, during my break, her escort for the evening, Eddie Bragno, who owned a fine wine shop on Walton & Rush, said, "Stanley, I'd like you to meet Ethel Merman."

Her first words to me were, **"Well, I'll be Goddamned. You certainly know all of my stuff. Christ, you even played the songs that got cut before they made it to Broadway!"**

That *voice!* I thought, "My God! She's even louder in person!" I was certain that when Merman spoke the deaf could turn off their hearing aids.

"Ya know, I'm opening tomorrow night at

the Empire Room at the Palmer House. So why don'tcha come by to see my show?"

The next night, arriving a little after the show began, I stood in the back of the room. She finished to a deserved standing ovation. I was getting ready to leave when she walked up to me and said, **"Hey you! Piano player from the Pump Room. You can tell 'em I'm leavin'! They can get another girl singer! That Goddamn light was makin all them cracklin noises,"** she yelled. **"And this F_ _ _ ING cordless mike they stuck in me is getting all kinds of feedback!"**

I wondered who had the brilliant idea to mike Ethel Merman in the Empire Room? You probably wouldn't need to give her a microphone in Soldier Field!

Her conductor, Stan Freeman, was an acquaintance of mine from the Henry Hermann days. "Stanley, how's it going?" he asked. Merman immediately bellowed, **"So it's *Stanley* is it? Well, I'm having a few people up to my suite so come on up and join us."**

"Thanks Miss Merman, I'd love to." I said.

"What's with the *Miss Merman?*" she shouted. **"It's *Ethel!*"**

When we got to the suite, we tried to calm her down but she started tugging on her gown and rearranging things. **"Ya *see*, it goes through my bra! Through my foundation, through everything, ya know!"** Then she proceeded to demonstrate exactly where the cordless mikes wandered. I couldn't believe it. Within less than fifteen minutes of arriving in her suite, we were not only on a first-name basis, but she was even showing me her underwear!

A few days later my phone rang. Holding the receiver about two feet from my ear, I could hear that unique yell, **"It's Ethel. I'm supposed to go to this Goddamn fancy dinner party. It's at that joint in the basement next to your hotel, so why don'tcha tag along for the ride?"**

That "joint in the basement" was Maxim's, probably the most glamorous restaurant in Chicago in the 1960s. It was a place known for the table settings with perfect, magnificent flowers, the great vintage wine and the French meals served with perfect sauces.

Three minutes after our entrees arrived, Merman began poking me in the ribs and whispering, if you can imagine a Merman whisper, **"Ya know, I can't stand this French crap they're serving. Gallo Chablis is *my* cup of tea, and you don't hafta try and get that damn cork out either. Ya just screw off the top and drink it!"**

The Gallo brothers never used her as a spokesperson. I wonder why? Yes, there was only one Ethel Merman!

FRED ASTAIRE

"I WON'T DANCE!"

I was half asleep when the telephone rang one morning. "Hi dear, it's Loosh! How would you like to play a party we're giving for Fred Astaire next week in the Sarah Siddons room? Hold on dear, would you?"

On the town with Ethel Merman.

"*Fred Astaire*!" I exclaimed. Too late, my caller already immersed in another conversation before I had a chance to open my mouth.

"Oh hi Stella, tell Kup I've got an exclusive for him. Have him give me a call as soon as he can, would you? Thanks dear," she said, just as another phone started ringing. "Lucia Perrigo." she answered. "Dorothy! Thanks for getting back to me. The article's perfect as is, but put an 'e' at the end of 'Astair,' okay? Great."

Lucia Perrigo, the Ambassador Hotels' public relations dynamo, usually had two or three phone conversations going on at the same time. In those days, Chicago had four daily newspapers and it was her job, assisted by Audrey Adams, to service all of them with newsworthy items, making sure the Pump Room and the hotels maintained a high visibility news profile, which they did!

"Stanley! Sorry about that," she said, rushing through her words as always. "I have to run now dear, but I'll fill you in later, all right? Be sure to brush up on your Astaire!" she added, and was gone.

Fred Astaire was coming to the Ambassador! What would I play? I went from a sleepy haze to wide awake in an instant. I immediately started going through my record collection. We played Fred and Ginger tunes nightly as a matter of course, songs like *Cheek to Cheek, The Way You Look Tonight*, you name it. But if I really wanted to impress Mr. Astaire, and I most certainly did, I had a lot of homework to do.

In less than an hour I had showered and dressed, and gotten myself down to the Chicago Public Library, looking for everything I could find about Fred Astaire and his music. Much of what I read I already knew, but I was surprised to learn that his very first on-screen dance partner was Joan Crawford! I didn't know she even danced.

My next stops were Chicago's premiere music stores, Lyon & Healy and the Carl Fisher Music Store, to collect sheet music. By mid-afternoon I was armed with enough Astaire material to create a 24-hour marathon of tunes from *Top Hat, Flying Down to Rio, Holiday Inn* and too many others to name. For the next few days my orchestra and I did nothing but learn the Astaire song books.

On the day of the party, we had been playing for about twenty minutes when our guest of honor arrived. A hush fell over the room and then endless applause followed, as everyone stood to welcome him. He shyly smiled, embarrassed, it seemed, more than anything else, and then began greeting people.

We started playing *Cheek to Cheek* while everyone formed a receiving line, waiting to be introduced to the *Legend*. He was busy shaking hands, smiling, and saying a few words to each of the individuals he met. Gracious, poised, every bit the gentleman we'd come to know on the silver screen. He spent a good deal of time chatting with one woman in particular, Carola Mandel, the widow of the man who founded the Mandel Brothers Department Store, Colonel Leon Mandel. She and her husband had been great friends of the late Ernie Byfield, creator of the Pump Room. Still a great beauty, the Pump

Fred Astaire with vivacious Carola Mandel—He never danced a step!

Room had named a house specialty after her, a soup they called *Cubana Carola.*

After about an hour of socializing, many of the guests had taken to the dance floor while Mr. Astaire continued to be wholly engaged in conversations. I doubted that he'd even noticed the tribute we'd been playing for him. And there was a further disappointment. I had imagined how great it would be to be able to say that Fred Astaire once danced to my orchestra! But on and on we played. Dozens of women were standing near him so obviously wanting to be his partner, and not once did he ask anyone to dance.

Just before the party broke up, to my amazement he made his way up to the bandstand and spoke to me. "Mr. Paul?" he said softly, leaning forward. "I just wanted to be sure to tell you how much I've enjoyed your rendition of my songs. Some of those I haven't heard since I danced to them with my sister, Adele, too many years ago to even think about!" He smiled, and extended his hand.

Fred Astaire was shaking my hand! That certainly offset any disappointment I'd felt about his not having danced a single step.

Years later I mentioned the incident to Essee Kupcinet, and she immediately shared her Fred Astaire "won't dance" story. She explained that one night, when Fred Astaire was visiting with the Kupcinets in their booth, the band started playing *"Shall We Dance."* Essee was quite the accomplished dancer, having studied for many years. There she was with the man, the music and the moment which could fulfill a fantasy of a lifetime.

She turned to Astaire and said, "For the better portion of my life I have prayed for just one thing, to have the opportunity to dance with Fred Astaire. I'll die if I don't dance with you."

Astaire sadly shook his head and gently gave her the bad news, "Essee, alas, you'll be among the dead, I am most sorry to say. Please forgive me, but I must decline."

She was speechless, shattered, and could only stare at him in disbelief. "Please take no offense," he added. "I am certain you are a fine dancer. But if I dance with you in a public place like this, can you imagine what my life would be like every time I came here? Or went to any public place with a dance floor, for that matter?"

JUDY GARLAND

AT THE END OF THE RAINBOW

Though my acquaintance with Judy Garland was a brief one, it was powerful in a lot of ways and an experience I will never forget. She was an incredible talent, and her death was one of the world's most tragic losses. Such an incredible waste.

My first glimpse of Judy Garland came in the spring of 1967. It was late in the afternoon, and there'd been a big rainstorm. The basement was flooded and the elevators weren't working. "She's coming down!" the assistant manager, Danny Sullivan, kept running through the lobby warning, nearly breathless. "And she's *hungry!*"

She was wearing a big hat, and had just gracefully descended sixteen flights of stairs. Garland was seated in Booth One, of course, but the funny thing was she wasn't the least bit out of breath. She was laughing about the whole experience! Like a kid who'd just been allowed to do something totally out of the ordinary for a change.

She'd stopped in Chicago on her way back to New York from L. A., where she'd just been fired from *Valley of the Dolls.* It would turn out to be her last movie offer, but no one knew that then.

A few months later, Judy Garland was back at the Pump Room after her opening night in the Civic Opera House. Her voice was just a whisper of what it once was, but audiences everywhere went wild every time she opened her mouth. The unspoken questions were always there, though. Will she make it? Will she even show up, let alone perform? It was her last concert in Chicago. A year and a half later, she'd be gone

She was a legend whose reputation had followed her, along with her fame. And now history and expectation were mixed together in a sort of frenzied way when people thought about Judy Garland. Sadness and admiration, along with an undeniable affection, and a hope that her tomorrows would be better than her todays. It was hard to explain. But there wasn't another performer alive who could generate those kinds of feelings from an audience. Even the Pump Room felt warmer while she was sitting in it.

I struck up the band as she walked into the room, and played all of her songs, even adding some of the special combinations of songs that she did. She wasn't in Booth One that night because there were too many people who wanted to be with her. She was seated at a long table set up in the center of the room, along with Irv and Essee Kupcinet, several newspaper critics and lots of people she seemed to know.

She sent a note to the bandstand thanking me for remembering her songs. "What happiness you are bringing me tonight," it said, and it is a memento I'll always cherish.

I stopped at her table during a break. She was telling stories and she was so animated! I was several seats away from her and couldn't hear very well, but when she mentioned the name Noel Coward my ears perked up. She was talking about a party they were at together, and then all of a sudden she sounded like Barbara Walters! No, it was an impression of Marlene Dietrich!

Judy was saying that Marlene, who always pronounced the letter "r" as if it was a "w," had asked the crowd if they'd care to hear her "we-cord." It was a recording of segments of a tour she'd just finished, apparently, but from what I could gather it was just Marlene's voice saying the name of some city, followed by applause.

"No music. No singing." Judy was saying. "Just *Haaam*-burg . . . applause for two minutes. *Wee*-o . . . applause for two minutes. *Aaam*-ster-*daaam* . . . applause for two minutes. One city after another . . . applause, applause, applause!"

Everyone at the table had quieted down to listen by now, captivated by Judy's performance. "We sat there for nearly half an hour before the damn thing finally ended!" she continued. "But Marlene? She was riveted! Riveted, I tell you!"

"Now tell them what Noel Coward said to you!" someone who'd obviously heard the story before suggested.

She turned herself into Noel Coward then, sitting up straight, raising her eyebrows and whispering in a deep throated English accent, "I *hope* there's not another side!" Then she looked around the table, lowered her head, and said in her own voice "But there *was*!", and the table exploded with laughter!

What an incredible mimic she was! As I looked around the table at all the laughing faces I knew she couldn't possibly be as sad and depressed as the press seemed to have made her out to be.

The next evening was a Friday, and Garland was back at the same table with just as many people. Sid Luft, her ex-husband, was managing the tour and was with her every night. So was Bobby Cole, her conductor. When things wound down around one o'clock, I was invited up to Judy's suite! She was going to listen to her *Judy at the Palace* recording that had just been released that day.

The hallway outside her door smelled like a flower shop, the fragrance growing stronger as we approached. And once inside, it was like a scene from Al Capone's funeral! Every flower in Chicago had to have been collected and sent to her suite! And there were stacks of telegrams and letters all over the place.

She walked over to the phonograph and put on the record, then took a seat on the floor and invited us to join her. When the music started to play everyone was sitting around her in a semi-circle offering congratulatory comments while she just cocked her head to one side and listened. I was curious about her own reaction to the recording. She never said a word, but her expression said that she was aware that she'd sounded better in the past. And there was the sadness. I realized it wasn't a figment created by the press after all.

What struck me most as the evening wore on was how tiny she was, how frail she looked with the dark circles under her eyes. She seemed so tired. Why I hadn't seen it before I'm not really sure, except that she was, after all, a performer. And that's what performers do, isn't it? Create illusions. I couldn't help but think that it was unfortunate that Judy Garland was trying to live hers.

At about 2:30 in the morning it was as though a bell went off that everyone heard but me. Sid left and went back to his room, then Bobby Cole stood up, said he was tired and started to leave. I'd figure out much later that they kept her company well into the wee hours of every morning on the road because she couldn't bear to be alone. And me? Without any advance agreement on my part, I was the relief for tonight at least. I was completely in awe of Judy Garland and loving every minute of my time with her!

"Stay and have a drink with me, Stanley." she pleaded, sounding so much like a little girl when she said it. "I'm not even close to tired yet."

"Oh my *God!*" I thought. "What am I going to talk about?" Then I spotted a little spinet piano in the corner of her suite and sat down and started playing. She walked Bobby Cole to the door, then crossed the room and lit up a cigarette. She took a big puff, sat down beside me and started to sing. They were the softest, whispered melodies, perfectly in tune and simply beautiful! I couldn't believe that I was sitting there beside her while she was singing so intimately to me. I was entranced.

"If only she'd sounded like this on her recording," I thought, but studios weren't big on recording whispering those days. I'd give anything now to have a tape of the way she sang that night.

She reached up to take another puff of her cigarette, and for the first time I noticed the slash marks on her wrist like a bracelet made of thin red scars. I kept playing as though nothing had happened, but she sensed the change in me as I sat there flash frozen.

She said nothing, just looked at me and inhaled what was left of her cigarette. How wet her eyes were! Great brown discs on their hazy white background, just looking right through me. Ghostlike somehow. And I just kept on playing as though it were background music to a dramatic scene on a movie screen in our minds.

Something almost ethereal passed between us in those instants. Understanding, I guess. An unspoken explanation that spoke more clearly than any words possibly could, and then a smile began in the corners of her mouth and slowly made its way across her face. She started singing again, a little louder than before but just as clearly, and for over an hour we stayed there at the piano lost in the music.

I'd start a song and she'd chime in, or "Stanley, do you know this Gershwin song?" she'd ask excitedly, every now and then. I eventually figured out that music was a refuge for her, that music stilled whatever demons roamed within. I was never more grateful than I was that night to have learned all those songs so many years before.

People ask me if she was drinking all the time, if there were drugs, and so on. Well, the truth is, there were a few watered down vodka and tonics around, but she was never drunk. And she never took any drugs that I saw. She did disappear into the john pretty often though, and I suspected she was probably taking some sort of pills, but I never saw anything first hand, so I can't really say for sure. At five in the morning she was still wide awake while I was in a semi-conscious daze, completely exhausted.

Finally, she got up from the piano and wandered over to the couch "to rest for a bit," she said. "Could you get one of my robes out of the closet over there?" she asked, pointing toward the open doors across the room.

I was shocked when I looked inside. There was only one robe in that closet, worn, pink and a little shabby. And there were two dresses, both very neatly placed on padded hangers, but one with a button missing from its sleeve. The saddest sight of all was the pair of shoes set down carefully on the floor just inside the closet door, scuffed in places, one with its buckle nearly torn off. Other than that, the closet was empty.

I brought the robe back to her, but she'd already curled herself into a corner of the couch and fallen asleep. Such childlike innocence. So vulnerable. I covered her with her robe as though it were a blanket, and made my way to the door.

She returned to the Pump Room the next night and was seated in Booth One, this time with Sid, Bobby, and two of her children, Lorna and Joey. They were part of the show and had accompanied her on this tour. She excused herself and took the children upstairs after dinner, promising to return when they were asleep. Lorna was about thirteen at the time, and Joey somewhere near ten.

"You mean those kids were sleeping last night while we were listening to records?" I asked just after she'd left. "While we played the piano until nearly dawn!"

"Sure!" Sid answered me. "By now they could sleep through a hurricane!"

Judy Garland came back down just after midnight and then, just like the previous evening, after my last set I was invited back to her suite. This time she put her famous concert of 1961, *Judy at Carnegie Hall,* on the record player. She'd never sounded better and preferred it, I suspected, to hearing her voice in its present condition.

After about an hour, Sid and Bobby left as they had the night before, and I suggested we go to my suite instead of hers this time. It was just a

With Judy at the entrance to the Pump Room.

few floors down and I had a grand piano. "We could really have some fun singing and playing." I said. The truth was I felt uncomfortable making such a racket with kids sleeping on the other side of the wall, whether they could sleep through hurricanes or not.

In my suite there were no reminders of her life's sadness. We both preferred it, I think, and time passed much more quickly than it had the previous evening. Her fabulous voice whispering its wonderful melodies in my very own suite just for me. We spent hours going through my collection of fake books, which contain only the melodies, chords and lyrics of songs as a guideline for professional musicians. It was the thrill of a lifetime and one I'll never forget.

It was nearly seven in the morning when I escorted her back up the elevator to her suite. She had to get up "fairly early," she said, because she was going to sing for the guys at the Great Lakes Naval Air Station in just a few hours. *Fairly* early! It was already fairly early! "Did she never sleep?" I kept asking myself.

I was out like a light the minute my head hit the pillow, and I didn't get up again until two o'clock in the afternoon. When I asked at the front desk just what time it was that Judy Garland had actually left the hotel, I was told she'd walked out the door at 10:30 that morning! I couldn't believe it!

I showed up for work at the Pump Room that night literally dragging myself onto the bandstand. And once again, Judy Garland was there with a small group for dinner, including the star of *Music Man*, Forrest Tucker. "Come up for a drink," she offered as usual, just around closing time, adding "We're leaving tomorrow, though, so it'll have to be an early night."

Early night! It was 1:30 a.m. already early morning. Half the city had been asleep for hours, and she wanted to make it an *early night?* That night, about fifteen minutes after everyone left her suite I made my excuses, "I'll be going then, too. You'll want to get some sleep before you catch that flight in the morning."

Judy had no intention of calling it a night, "Whaddaya mean? You just *got* here, Stanley. And you *have* to hear Liza's new album! Tell me

what you think?" We listened, as I stared off somewhere into space, forcing myself to stay awake.

"Did I ever tell you about the Gumm sisters?" she said when the record ended. For the next half hour she told one hysterical story after another about her childhood days when she and her sisters were in Vaudeville. She accompanied every story by singing and dancing around the room. I was way beyond tired by then. To this day I can't remember a single one of those stories, but I do remember that I never laughed as heartily before or since, as I did with her that night!

It was nearly four thirty in the morning before I finally persuaded her to try to get a little rest. I went

CHICAGO TRIBUNE, TUESDAY, SEPTEMBER 19, 1967

TOWER TICKER
By Herb Lyon

THE HOT LYON: Judy Garland's new Big Romance is Pump Room Maestro Stan Paul: Judy spent Sat. and Sun. warbling 'til 8 a.m. to Stan's snappy piano playing in his suite with her entourage in tow—Judy's best show of all! The comeback gal also cheered wounded Viet Nam GIs Sun. at Great Lakes hosp....

(© Copyrighted Chicago Tribune Company. All rights reserved, used by permission.)

down to my suite and put a Do Not Disturb sign on the knob, closed the door behind me and slept through much of Monday. About 8 a.m. on Tuesday morning, the phone kept ringing until I reluctantly answered it. "Have you seen the Tribune?" a friend was screaming excitedly. "You and Judy Garland are the lead item in Herb Lyon's column!"

The never to be forgotten Judy Garland.

Wherever I went for the next few weeks someone would start humming *Somewhere, Over the Rainbow,* or kiddingly ask how the "big romance" was going. I never told anyone that the whole experience was exhausting. The truth is, one more week of "Dorothy" and I'd have been over the rainbow myself!

JIMMY DURANTE

TAKING KINDNESS TO A NEW LEVEL

"Good night Mrs. Calabash, wherever you are."

Anyone who's ever been a Jimmy Durante fan will recognize those words because they ended

The Schnoze was Jerry Lewis' idol.

every radio and TV show he ever did—and there were a lot of them! I remember laughing at the great 'Schnozzola' on the radio when I was just a little kid, and that was before I'd ever even seen that nose!

He was a comfortable kind of comedian, a natural. The kind that could make any words funny just by saying them. And I loved his songs! Later, when I actually got a look at him, he was even funnier! He always seemed to enjoy himself so much with that wonderful gravely voice and the fedora perched on the side of his head. Everyone loved Jimmy Durante. How could you not? So when I finally met him face to face years later in the Pump Room, I felt as though I'd known him all my life.

He brought his old partner, Eddie Jackson, with him. We played his theme song *Inka Dinka Doo* and when I walked past their booth Mr. Durante thanked me and invited me to "take a seat." He was so soft spoken! I was surprised, having only heard his 'on stage' voice.

"Ya know, I use ta play pi-aaaa-na at parties in my *young*-er days!" he grinned at me later, and told me about a few of the gigs he did on the Lower East Side. I told him about how I started out in New York, and we discovered we had a lot in common.

"*Every* night's party night around dis place, ain't it?" he growled the words through a grin. "One a da tings I liked about da twennies."

"The 1920s?" I asked.

"Ahh yaahhh . . . da twennies! I owned a *speak-easy* den an' I gotta tell ya, it was heaven!"

"Da Pump Room's a little tamer," he smiled then, lowering his voice to a whisper in that funny way he had of pretending to be greatly disappointed. "So Eddie! Tell 'im 'bout da good ol' days!" he said then, winking at me, "No-bo-dy knows 'em like Eddie!"

This is a scene that repeated itself often on Jimmy's visits to the Pump Room. He made a point of making sure Eddie was always included in the conversation. It had been years since he'd needed his old partner in his act, but he kept him on, nonetheless. I can't remember ever meeting a nicer and kinder man than Jimmy.

JOAN CRAWFORD

JOANIE DEAREST

One afternoon, I was having lunch at The Greenery, the coffee shop which was located on the

Two fashion icons—Joan Crawford and style editor Peg Zwecker.

Ambassadors' basement level, when the head housekeeper came bounding through the entrance, huffing and puffing and waving sheets of paper in the air. She grabbed the stool next to mine and started talking before she even sat down. "Can you *imagine?* Now she's demanding an armed security guard to be stationed outside her

suite! Day and night, no less! For what? Nobody even knows who she is anymore. So how's her life in danger? *God!* Where does she dream these things up?"

Of course I knew *exactly* who she was talking about. Only one guest in the world ever inspired that sort of tirade from the housekeeping staff. "So when's Miss Joan Crawford arriving?" I asked with a smile.

"Day after tomorrow," she confided, shaking her head and spreading the three sheets of paper she'd been waving around out onto the counter in front of me. "Just look at this, Stanley! Three single spaced, typewritten pages of these *requests* of hers!"

I can remember a few of them:

- the suite must be filled with flowers

- one dozen down pillows for her bed

- special linens, woven with a thread count no lower than 360 per square inch

- every single known brand of aerosol spray air freshener

- a detailed list of cleaning supplies, with special attention to disinfectants

- case of Pepsi (out of deference to her husband, who ran the Pepsi-Cola organization)

- Miss Crawford must never run out of 100 proof vodka

I was just the piano player and never had to deal with any of her outlandish demands, so I used to love it when she came to the hotel. I never knew another star who could stir people up the way she did and on top of that, she was fascinating to watch. All her moves so melodramatic.

When she was in Booth One, she was always on at least one telephone. On one occasion, Kup found

The always glamourous Joan Crawford.

himself tangled in the cords from the three telephones she was using simultaneously at the table. "Joanie," he finally said, "you've got to stop talking. It looks like we're eating at a table filled with spaghetti!"

By the time I met her, her last husband, Alfred Steele, major domo of Pepsi-Cola, had died and her movie career, or what was left of it, was nearly over. Her last four pictures were quick thrillers, cheap and sleazy. She took them seriously, though, as she took everything. In Joan's mind, she was still the big movie star and still demanded to be treated like one.

A few years later, shortly before I left the Pump Room, she was back. Only this time, she was all alone seated in Booth One. During one of my breaks, I went by to say hello and she invited me to sit with her. She still looked glamorous and couldn't have been nicer. As we talked, she sipped from a large water glass. At least I assumed the glass was filled with water until Victor, the maitre d', revealed that Miss Crawford always demanded and got 100-proof vodka without ice. Her "water" could knock out a Cossack.

But it seemed a little sad that she was all alone. Her last film, a low budget potboiler called *"Trog,"* had been released a few years before.

As I left the booth and walked back toward the bandstand, I thought to myself, "Is this how it all ends, one of the greatest film stars of her generation sitting in solitary glamour in an otherwise empty Booth One?"

HERMOINE GINGOLD

TRUE GOLD

Hermione Gingold, who was a star because of her personality and outrageous sense of humor, was a very special friend, and remained so for many years. She lived in New York, but traveled back and forth between the coasts quite a lot filming TV shows, or the occasional movie. She was terrified of flying, and always took the train from one place to the other. Just like the stars of Byfield's era, she made a point of stopping off in Chicago for a day or two on each trip, staying at the Ambassador East Hotel and dining in the Pump Room, of course!

Prior to one memorable trip, she had injured her hip and asked me to meet her at the train sta-

My zany wonderful friend Hermione Gingold.

tion. When she got off the train, she was limping severely. And she was carrying a tiny Yorkshire terrier in her arms with a cast on its leg! The dog's name was Missy (nicknamed Messy Missy by the hotel housekeeping staff for obvious reasons), and she accompanied Miss Gingold on all her trips.

"Even trips to hospital!" Miss Gingold explained, as she and the dog hobbled through the station. What a sight it was! The two of them limping along, while the porter trailed behind with a mountain of luggage that included a collection of wigs stored in hat boxes of all different sizes which were on the verge of tumbling down onto the pavement at any moment. If that wasn't enough, she started singing a song from a new Broadway musical, Michael Butler's *Hair,* which had just opened on Broadway the previous week.

She insists I learn, "**It is the daw-ning of the A-a-a-age of A-quar-eee-ous! A-a-a-ge of A-quar-eee-ous! A-quaaaaar-eeeee-ous!!!**"

I walked along just a little behind so she wouldn't notice that I was hardly able to *contain* myself! The whole spectacle was like a scene from a Marx Brothers movie, and on this particular occasion, I must admit that Hermione bore a striking resemblance to Harpo!

A few years later the movie *Myra Breckenridge* had just been released, and Hermione, who was in town, called to say she was "dying to see it. Mae West is in it, Stanley. Mae *West!*" she kept insisting, as though that were reason enough for anyone to be persuaded.

I met her in the lobby later that same day, and we climbed into a taxi on our way to the loop. Just

as we started moving along I heard this yelp and this little, brownish-gray, furry head poked out from her handbag and looks up at me!

"Great!" I thought to myself. "We're going to get thrown out of that theater for sure if they see that face!" But they'd hear it before they saw it. Missy was a tiny dog, but you wouldn't believe the racket she could raise!

I bought the tickets, we went into the theater and the movie started. So far, so good. But when the 'nearly eighty year old Mae West looking like an embalmed Jean Harlow made her appearance on the screen, Hermione let out a shriek! In an instant the dog was out of the handbag, off her lap and bolting down the aisle full speed.

People are starting to murmur as Missy scrambled under the seats on one side of the theater and then the next. Heads were bobbing up and down all over the place as people jumped to their feet to get out of her way. Hermione was on all fours herself, screaming, "Missy! Where are you? Come back my little darling!"

Eventually, Missy tired of running all over the place and came prancing back up the aisle towards us, tail wagging. Was she chastised? Was the dog given just the tiniest indication of disapproval or perhaps a moment of discipline? Of course not! Instead Missy was scooped up into Hermione's arms immediately and smothered with some very noisy kisses. As could only be expected, we were asked to leave the theater.

I never wanted to see the damn movie anyway!

CHAPTER NINE

WINDS OF CHANGE

I spent a lot of time with celebrities and movie stars looking back on their lives. I'd try to imagine the times they talked about, and it wasn't always easy. Times change. Nothing lasts forever. Thoughts like this crossed my mind now and then, though only rarely. I was too busy living my whirlwind existence, caught up in all the excitement.

It seemed like half of the celebrities in the twentieth century passed through my suite during those years. And the schedule never altered much from one day to the next, as weeks turned into months turned into years. Many nights various stars stayed in my suite until three or four in the morning, and I'd think nothing of running to Milano's on Division Street at that hour for pizza. Or to the Little Rock Garden on Clark Street near Division for Chinese food. It was often five in the morning before I'd be heading home for the night, but usually, I didn't have to be up until one in the afternoon. The housekeeping staff put my room off till the end of their shift, and the maid would rattle her keys outside my door as a signal that she was nearly ready.

My jingling alarm clock would awaken me except on the days when the telephone would ring first. Nena Ivon from Sak's Fifth Avenue ran the fashion shows at the Pump Room on Tuesdays and Thursdays. If she was on the phone, it meant I had exactly forty-five minutes to be downstairs and seated behind the piano, ready to start the show.

"Do you want bacon and eggs, or pancakes?" she'd begin sweetly, and I'd stumble over myself to get to the shower. On most afternoons, however, I wasn't working, and I still loved to wander around the city exploring, but now usually with friends. In the evenings when I wasn't playing in the Pump Room, I caught the acts of visiting celebrities whenever possible. I might catch the show at the Camellia House in the Drake Hotel, where the orchestra leader Dick Judson was a good friend, or run over to the Consort Room of the Hotel Continental Plaza, where Franz Benteler and his Royal Strings held forth.

Around this time, I remember reading in the paper that Sally Rand would be appearing at Mangam's Chateau in Lyons. I hadn't seen her since that night when I played for her when I was 16 years old. I couldn't believe that she could still be dancing.

On opening night, just as coffee was being served the room went dark and the voice over the microphone announced: "Mrs. Helen Mangam presents . . . the legend herself . . . Miss Sally *Rand!*"

Suddenly, all the lights came back on and the whole stage was bathed in deep blue light.

With all the smoke in the air, it created a very eerie atmosphere. And then this vision appeared! Two huge ostrich feather fans, blond hair up swept, and two tiny feet with plastic high heels without backs, twirling these two huge fans around the stage as she very gracefully performed her famous fan dance. The same song, *Claire de Lune*, was playing over a scratchy phonograph instead of a piano. I couldn't believe it! Nothing had changed one bit since that night that I'd played for her!

"Stanley!" a familiar voice called out as she approached our table. "I saw your name on the reservation list. It's good to see you!" It was the owner, Helen Mangam. She was also the mother of a good friend of mine, Joan Wegner, whom I'd known forever! As a matter of fact, Joan and her husband, Chuck, were there at my first opening night at the Pump Room in 1964. She was in her training diamonds in those years!

"Would you care to meet Miss Rand?" she offered.

"Of course!" and just a few moments later out she came. She'd changed out of her costume or

Lucia Perrigo, Sally Rand and me. Lucia asked Sally to bring her fans for a photo shoot in my apartment. Next to Lucia, a vintage 1940s juke box that I paid 25 bucks for—I only wish I still had it.

whatever it was that she actually wore under those fans, a nude body stocking, some people said. When she finally got to the table she was very sweet. I explained that I'd once played the piano for her. That night I finally got a chance to tell her, "And lady, you still owe me ten bucks!"

Five days later we met in Booth One of the Pump Room. She wore a plain red suit and a little hat, looking very much like any lady in those days who might be lunching at the Pump Room. Then I looked down. She was wearing black fish-net stockings and clear plastic shoes, what they used to call Spring-o-laters. When she noticed that I was staring at her legs and feet, she said, "Remember honey, I *am* Sally Rand!"

Lunch turned out to be a lot of fun! I asked her how she'd gotten started in show business. She said she'd been knocking around for years, but she hadn't made much progress of her own at all. She'd made some silent movies in Hollywood in the 1920s, but her career was not going anywhere. In 1933, she was working at the Club Paramount on Huron Street but she wanted to get a job as a dancer at Chicago's 1933 World's Fair, the Century of Progress, they called it.

"It was impossible to get someone to talk to you, let alone get an audition." she explained. "Then I read in the papers that there was going to be this big society party at the Street of Paris exhibit on the fairgrounds the night before opening day and I decided to *crash* it!" she exclaimed, her eyes dancing.

Having crashed the "Lolita" premiere several years before, I immediately recognized that Sally Rand and I were publicity soul mates.

She said she rented a horse for the night, and paid a guy who had a barge docked on the Chicago River to bring her to the fair. "It cost just about my last ten dollars, too!" she added. She covered her nudity with switches of hair she tied around herself, climbed up on the horse and rode it to the Streets of Paris exhibit, where the party was already well underway. She was an immediate sensation, a bigger hit than the original Lady Godiva. The photographers went wild. Remember, it was 1933 and you just didn't see a nude woman out in public very often. And on a horse no less!

Anyway, she went back to her job at the Club Paramount that night, and then to the inexpensive rooming house on Division Street were she was living. She got up early the next day, took a trolley back to the World's Fair and, for the first time, picked up the newspaper.

"My photograph was plastered all over the pages! And the headlines were screaming all about *'Lady Godiva on a Horse!'*" she giggled. She told the man at the gate of the Streets of Paris that she was the same girl that was all over the papers, and he told her to get her costume and come right back! She didn't need the horse any more!

Sally Rand concluded, "So I ran back and grabbed the two fans that I danced with at the club and I've been doing that same dance for the past thirty-five years!"

That was in 1968 and summer in Chicago that year revolved around the Democratic National Convention. It was held here the last week in August, but preparations had been going on months in advance. It was the biggest media event Chicago had seen in years, and everyone was excited about it.

I could hardly wait to meet Walter Cronkite!

The first week about five thousand young people showed up in the city, kids people referred to as hippies. Most were from the suburbs, some from local universities, a few were professional agitators.

They were young, that's all I knew about it. And a few hundred of them set up an encampment in Old Town, less than a mile from the Ambassador East. Most just played their guitars and did a lot of singing, but some were handing out pamphlets and making a lot of speeches that only the other hippies

seemed to be listening to. It didn't seem frightening at all, just different.

The out of town press started arriving on Friday, and a full contingent was based in the hotel from that point forward. It was as though a big city newspaper had been recreated in the Pump Room. People on phones, getting up from tables, rushing back and forth dodging wagons just to say something important to a group at another table. Everyone was talking so fast and saying so much! On a walk from the bandstand to the front door after a set, I'd hear an opinion on the war in Viet Nam, a comment on unrest in Czechoslovakia, and someone might rush in with an urgent message about something that just happened in Grant Park.

It was exciting having so many correspondents there all the time, to be able to get a behind-the-scenes look at it all this way. And every once in awhile I'd recognize someone who'd stopped by, Chet Huntley and David Brinkley, John Chancellor, Eric Sevareid and, yes, I actually did get to meet Walter Cronkite! And Gore Vidal too, as a matter of fact.

Frank Sinatra arrived on Sunday afternoon, and took the same four-room suite he always did, the one Joe Kennedy used when he stayed in Chicago years ago. Mrs. Martin Luther King, a grieving widow whose husband had been killed in Memphis only four months before, was also staying at the hotel.

Perle Mesta, the world famous hostess from Washington, D.C., was not only staying at the Ambassador, but came to the Pump Room constantly!

She'd sit, jewel-laden and gowned, having dinner in Booth One while I played *Hostess With the Mostest* from *Call Me Madam,* the Irving Berlin musical loosely based on her life. Mrs. Mesta made a point of always coming up to the bandstand personally to thank me for playing her song. Then she'd have her dinner, go upstairs and take a

Perle Mesta's diamond necklace could have paid off the national debt!

nap. A few hours later, she'd reappear in a completely different gown, and run through the whole scene again! I'd play her song, she'd come up to the bandstand to thank me, have another dinner, then go upstairs.

The Pump Room's regularly scheduled fashion show on Tuesday afternoon went off without a hitch, but all the media people were hovering around in the lobby, complaining bitterly to people on the other ends of telephones. The city was imposing a "news blackout" they insisted, that "security was being used as an excuse to restrict press access" and that "it was a form of harassment." It was so tight that even Pierre Salinger, former press officer for President Kennedy, couldn't get past police at the Conrad Hilton to give his own press conference! The press were fuming! Every hour that went by that day, the reporters' moods seemed to get darker, then in late afternoon, they all left to get their stories.

The Pump Room was quiet that night, a sharp contrast to the press room atmosphere of just hours before. People sat and silently ate their dinners, and when they left, few came in to take their places. It was dead and getting deader, strange for the Pump Room, even on a slow night. Victor signaled to let me know I had a message at the front

desk, so I ended the set and went out to the lobby to pick it up. It was from Mrs. Olmsted, a dear friend of mine who lived around the corner on Astor Street and was a frequent guest at the Pump Room. "Shut your windows so the tear gas won't get in!" the message read. "Tear gas?" I said out loud. "What is she talking about?"

"There's been a riot in Lincoln Park. Demonstrators and clergymen challenged the curfew!" a young reporter ran up the front stairs just then and announced. "The police attacked, sprayed them with tear gas to make them leave. You can really smell it if you go outside. But be careful, they're running past the hotel right now!"

I went outside and just stood there watching it with the door man, speechless. It was like watching a scene from a war movie play out in front of us. People, mostly kids and what looked like priests, were running and stumbling down State Street. A lot of them were hurt. Some were bleeding. And then, as I looked closer, I realized that someone had turned over a Rolls Royce that had been parked in front of the Churchill Hotel, just across the street! My God! What was happening?

I looked up for some reason then, that gesture we make when there's no answer here on earth. The sky was clear, and filled with stars. They looked so peaceful! So perfect. "The only stars around here tonight," I thought, so much more than disappointed.

From that point on, the whole convention experience went downhill. As exciting as everything still was, now instead of celebrating, we were part of a drama viewed by the world. Wednesday afternoon was much the same as the one before, just more somber, then the press cleared out around five o'clock. Again, attendance was light in the Pump Room, but later in the evening, I noticed what appeared to be a disturbance of some sort at the entrance. I cut the set short and walked over to see what was going on.

"Something's happened in Grant Park in front of the Hilton." Victor whispered. "It's been telecast, apparently. People are going upstairs to their rooms to watch it on their televisions."

I thanked him, and headed upstairs as fast as I could. On Channel 2, CBS, someone was making a speech on the convention floor. NBC was showing live coverage of the scene at Grant Park, where the police were trying to subdue the angry crowd. Police and demonstrators were obviously hurt. All I could see on television was mass confusion. Who ever would have thought this convention could turn out like this? I switched to channel eleven, Chicago's PBS station, which was broadcasting the ballet. WGN, the local station, was showing a 'Mr. Clean' commercial, but I wasn't too amused by the irony then.

When the reporters returned to the Ambassador that night, there was bedlam. Every telephone in the place was taken and correspondents were editing their broadcasts right there on the tables.

I was playing all night but nobody was listening. I could have been playing *The Star Spangled Banner* and I doubt anyone would have even noticed!

I'd been so excited to have met the politicians and social types that had come for the convention! I never expected *this!* The police had been prepared for it, everyone had been worried, but I hadn't a clue! I read the social columns, not the national news. It was the sixties and people my age were getting married in the park, smoking pot. The Grateful Dead were here, and I had no interest whatsoever in them. What did I care about Bob Dylan or Janis Joplin? Irving Berlin never wrote a musical for them.

What happened at that convention was an awakening, however rude. I'd worked hard to get where I was. I was proud of myself. By the summer of 1968 it became apparent that change was in the air. Some people sensed it, but a lot of people didn't—people like me. Martin Luther King was dead, and so was Robert Kennedy. The Viet Nam War had become a household word. They were major political events, happening far away, in another place. Life went on much the same as it ever had, in a day-to-day sense. In the Pump Room, nothing had really changed one bit.

It was the beginning of a nagging fear that I was missing something. That I didn't understand people my own age anymore! The world was changing and where was I? I was entertaining people a generation older, so caught up in what I was doing that I was missing everything else happening around me. Slowly, the realization began to alter my perspective.

I had a hard time understanding what it was that was happening. I understood the anti-war part of it. By the late sixties Viet Nam had divided the country. In fact, everything people were protesting about made no sense to me. It was confusing, more than it was anything else. I was where I'd always wanted to be, living a lifestyle I was happy with, more than happy! And it seemed that these kids wanted to take it away. They were making fun of it. As though walking around with no job, dirty clothes and long hair was an acceptable alternative. Acceptable for whom?

For the first time in my life, I felt *older*, not an altogether bad feeling either. I must admit that the dress code I was subject to probably contributed to it. I think it must have been a rule that you had to dress as a *grown up!* Blue jeans weren't allowed, never had been, and even in the late 1960's, they were simply unheard of in the Hotels Ambassador. Even if I was wearing them on my way *out* of the hotel, I had to dodge the lobby and sneak through the kitchen exit.

My process of discovering the world beyond the walls of the Pump Room was accelerated when a Tribune columnist brought a young girl to the Pump Room for lunch. She had just opened at Mr. Kelly's the night before and was second on the bill with comedian Jackie Vernon.

Her name was Bette Midler, and she'd played one of the three sisters in *Fiddler on the Roof,* and was about to appear at a place called The Continental Baths in New York City.

I went to see her that night at Mr. Kelly's. She was down right bawdy! She was fabulous! She wore 1930s evening gowns from thrift shops, and bounced around braless, singing songs like the Mae West classic *Come Up and See Me Sometime* and the 1950's *ShaBoom, ShaBoom,* and was cracking up the audience. She was alive and the room could feel it. The show was great and everyone knew it.

Her sense of humor was infectious and we hit it off right away. She was staying at the old Maryland Hotel on Delaware for around nine dollars a night. "She won't be for long," I thought to myself. We rode the bus together and hit every vintage clothing shop on Clark Street, spending virtually all the time talking and laughing. We compared stories about coming to New York for the first time, my trip from West Chester and hers from Hawaii.

(Photo courtesy of Steve Starr)
A young Bette Midler trying on vintage clothes at Steve Starr Studios on North Clark St.

As long as we stayed on the subject of past experiences and show tunes we were fine, but before very long she discovered that I knew nothing about what was currently happening musically. She'd mention pop stars of the day and, for the most part, I had no idea who any of them were! It was embarrassing. And she was amazed.

She went on and on about people whose music I'd never even heard of like Neil Young, Crosby, Stills & Nash, the Grateful Dead, Janis Joplin, Jimmy Hendrix. Did I like them?

"*Like* them!" I thought to myself. "Who *are* they?" Needless to say, I did not have the slightest idea who half the performers she mentioned were.

"Have you ever been to a concert, Stanley?" she asked. "A rock concert. Anybody's?"

"Well, no. Not actually," I had to admit. "I've seen the Beatles on Ed Sullivan. It seems more like amplifier noise than music to me."

"How 'bout the records, then? Ever buy anything current, like after 1940?"

"Each night in the Pump Room, I'm playing the music I like to hear!" I defended myself, "I'm surrounded with great music all the time!"

"*Hell!*" she snapped back at me. "I love it too! But that's not *all* there is! There's a lotta great stuff out there. I wanna keep in touch with what people are doin'. I wanna hear it *all!* Why don't you? You're not *part of* the older generation, ya know. You just play for 'em!"

The girl asked questions no one had ever asked. Questions I'd asked myself now and then, but only on some subconscious level, I think. Just doubts, never actual words.

"What would you do if the Pump Room closed, Stanley? The world's changin', ya gotta get with it!" were her last words on the subject.

She was right, though I didn't want to admit it. I tried not to think about what she'd said and to focus on the advantages of my situation instead of the negatives. I remembered that I'd collected quite a few autographed pictures of movie stars, and I decided to make copies as presents for my two nieces, Joanie and Sandy, the next time I went to the east coast for a family visit.

"Thank you, Uncle Stanley." they said politely, but with little excitement. They did request pictures of the Beatles, though, and asked if I knew them. It was obvious they had no idea who the people I considered stars even were. A generation apart. A different time. A different era. And there was that question again… "Where was I?"

Bette Midler's words made a lasting impression, that last bit of breeze that gets a rock rolling down a hill. "You really are in trouble." I told myself, and vowed to start doing something about it right away. But in actual practice, it was a very slow process for me.

I started buying newer records and started venturing to younger clubs to hear what was going on. I even went to Lincoln Park on Sundays to listen to long haired young people making speeches. I was trying to understand what this hippie thing was all about, slowly making the transition from apathy to . . . what? Awareness, if nothing else. I wasn't really sure where the questions would lead, but at least beginning to ask them.

Everything around me started to seem emptier, more shallow. The stars still came in, although there were fewer of them, as the theaters that catered to the so-called star system started closing. People didn't seem as interested as they once were in seeing an old movie star in a mediocre play just because she was famous.

I was constantly in a tug of war with myself. Sometimes I hated my suite and all my Pump Room surroundings and wanted to run off and explore the rest of the world. And other times I loved the excitement of a star's arrival in the room, entertaining them in my suite. I was ready for a change, but not ready to leave the Pump Room either. Something wasn't right, and I was nervous a lot of the time and not really happy.

Then someone from GRT Recording Company asked me to record a 'Country and Western' album of all things! Why, I've no idea, since I didn't play anything that sounded at all like country

I still think the best thing about the album was the cover. Left to right; Mitzi Magin, Hermione Gingold (seated on fender), Mamie Walton, Nicki Harris, Cynthia Olson, Susie Lennox, Barbara Weed, Donna Beaumont Atwater, Alita Murphy, Joan Braught.

"I look like the wrangler from Saks Fifth Avenue."

My last photo taken for the Pump Room, 1972.

music. "But why not?" I thought, since no one was exactly beating down my door offering a record contract at the time.

The album was called *The Jet Set Goes Country.* Looking back on it, I think the best thing about the whole project was the cover with Hermoine Gingold and a lot of Chicago socialites standing with me around a 1926 Rolls Royce. The record company even sent me to various country stations in the midwest to plug this turkey. When I arrived wearing my "country" costume, no one confused me with a cowboy. I looked like the wrangler from Saks Fifth Avenue.

After that, I took a much-needed vacation. I packed one bag, no tie, no jacket, and certainly no tuxedo, and went to California for a few weeks. It was a total change of scene, a complete break with what had become my routine. I relaxed. I thought about my life and about what was missing in it. I needed more exposure, to a group more diverse than the one I'd grown so attached to at the Pump Room. But at the same time, I didn't want to sub-

stitute one for the other. It was a dilemma. But after three weeks of consideration, I came back to Chicago with a few ideas.

The answer, I decided, was to start doing private bookings, play parties and start playing to a broader audience. But that wasn't something I could just jump into. I had to do this little by little, one step at a time. So when I renewed my contract with the hotel in August of 1971, I gave them notice that when it expired the following year, I wasn't planning to renew on the same terms. I wanted to limit my engagements to about four months per year after September of 1972.

I don't know why I was surprised that Kup was on the phone only four hours later. "You have a great position at the Pump Room! And steady! Where are you ever going to find a spot like that again? Think about that, Stanley," he warned.

But I had thought about it, long and hard. It was probably the most well thought out decision I'd made in my life. I was taking a risk, I understood that. But it was a risk I had to take. It was time. And I was ready.

I loved the Pump Room, and all the wonderful experiences I'd had there. Nothing could possibly replace the incredible memories I collected. It was a magical time, but times were changing, for all of us. And in September of 1972, I played my Pump Room Swan Song and made my exit.

My career emphasis immediately shifted to private bookings, though I wasn't able to put together an orchestra right away. With just a small combo, maybe five or six musicians at the most, I booked private parties and social events from a desk I set up at Associated Booking's offices in the Playboy Towers on Michigan Ave.

I had the occasional offer to play some of the bigger parties, the Summer Ball, September Ball, the Crystal Ball. But you had to be able to offer musicians a lot of work in order to keep a big orchestra together. Just starting out, I wasn't attracting enough business yet to support a big organization. As I'd known from the start, that would take time.

We started playing small parties at some of the private clubs like the Casino, the Standard Club, the Women's Athletic Club, and so on. Then Stanley and George Horwich of Weddings, Inc., started calling me to play a few weddings.

I played a party in New York, then one on the west coast, then before long a few engagements came in from around the country. It gave me a chance to travel, to get some exposure to other kinds of music and people with different musical tastes. It was a growing experience and long overdue.

I'd packed up my suite and put everything into storage in 1972, pending some decision as to where I'd ultimately settle down. I bought a small house in California, and commuted back and forth between gigs.

When I returned to Chicago, I did so as my own person, not in the "Pump Room Ambassador" role I'd filled for so long. I had a smaller suite, with just hotel furniture, none of my own, and all I kept there was some clothing and a few things I needed. There were no more late night parties. It was a monk-like existence compared to what had been. I was discovering a whole new Chicago and started making a new set of friends my own age.

I was beginning to get to know myself and to catch up on my life. And I'd grown a beard but shaved it, then side burns. I was thinking about growing the beard back, but who knew what I'd do tomorrow? I was flexible! More flexible than I'd ever been, and loving every minute of it. In between out-of-town engagements, I'd come back to the Pump Room for a four to six week run, which is where I was in May of 1973 when Bette Davis came to visit.

The Sarah Siddons Society, a local group supporting theater in Chicago, was presenting her with an "Actress for All Seasons Award," paying tribute to a remarkable career that in 1973 had spanned more than forty years on stage and screen. Miss Davis had flown into town the day before the gala, and it was no surprise to see her burst into the Pump Room for dinner the very night of her arrival. I'd been looking forward to it for weeks!

The basket I'd sent up to her suite that afternoon was just a 'hello' from an old friend. We'd exchanged notes and an occasional call during the course of the years, but I hadn't seen or talked to her for awhile. There was a lot to catch up on.

That night she made an entrance as only Bette Davis would or could! She burst upon the room and then held it enthralled. Dramatic gestures pouring out of her as though set on some auto-

"Start at the be-gin-ning Stanley Paul," she said.

matic pilot, she sat beside me on my piano bench singing.

"Start at the be-gin-ning, Stanleypaul," she'd said. Looking back on it now, there were quite a few beginnings, and there would be many more, each one with its own set of memories and consequences.

Arnold Morton, who had opened a restaurant named Arnie's, created an arrangement that would work well for both of us for several years. My contract with him gave me a lot of flexibility, something that was becoming more and more important to me. I could take off to play parties whenever I had a booking—and, thank goodness, the bookings were becoming more frequent.

The more parties I played, the more fun I was having. Thousands of parties later . . . but that is another book. I just thank my lucky stars that I was given the opportunity to be in the right room at the right time and for this I feel blessed.

I have lived the dreams of my youth. If there is anything to be learned from that I suppose it is that we should all have the dreams, do what is necessary to fulfill them and constantly figure out how to overcome the inevitable problems that are a part of any life.

The dance goes on.

A SALUTE FROM "THE LEADER OF A BIG-TIME BAND"

Cole Porter, "Something for the Boys," 1943

I have been most fortunate to have had the most talented musicians to support my endeavors from the moment I began my Chicago career at the Pump Room. Bob Woodville and Tom Beranek were two of my earliest associates. I then met Jack Hall, a fine trumpeter and arranger, who helped me organize a library of his charts, and expand my trio into a true band, complete with horns, percussion and even strings. The trio which formed shortly thereafter is still intact: Bob Berg on drums and Bernie Hunter on bass have been with me almost thirty years. They are the foundation upon which the band has grown.

Twenty-five years ago, Jack brought a trumpeter to work with us one night, and he has since become my associate conductor and my confidant. Jerry Norman has also written a large section of the library and is the leader of my other orchestra. Where Jack left off, Jerry has continued.

So many fine musicians have contributed to the Stanley Paul Orchestra. The saxophones of George Newquist, Frank Schalk and Chuck Kainz are silent now, but oh how they could play! Al Miller and Ray Nergaard keep it going. On trombone, where Lauren Binford and Bill Dinwiddie played, Ian Lilly has been our mainstay for 20 years. Fine trumpeters such as Boris Steffan, Steve Cooper, David Ruth, Rob Fund, Don Sohan and Bill Helmer have all contributed to the brass of the band.

Imagine the grand staircase of the flagship Chicago Hilton Hotel. As the guests ascend, the sounds of violins lead them into the festivities of the Grand Ballroom. Betty Monahan and her associates Joyce Marcheschi, Jodi Ferguson, Irene Quirmbach, Mark Hennessey, Joe Purpora, Ralph Boyd, Bob Lucas, Dan and Charlotte Bogda—to name a few— have given many events a touch of elegance!

Percussionists Bruce Nelson, Dede Sampaio and Rick Boetel have been invaluable. As my orchestra has changed with the decades, my guitarists have become so important. I have been fortunate to have John Nicholas, and now Paul Wood, to keep us current. Paul sings, writes, plays piano and takes command when the band boogies. Lino Frigo, from WGN, was with us for a long time on keyboard, and now we have Lee Noren, who continues to write for us and keep us on our toes.

I feel so fortunate to have two of the finest singers in Chicagoland in my band, Anne deLangis and Cindy Symmonds bring a sound to our group that people applaud and continually request. Anne and Cindy sound like "sisters" when they sing together. We call them "The Swing Sisters." Along with Paul Wood, we have a great front line.

Many, many thanks, and may the song continue for many years!

Stanley Paul

SPECIAL THANKS

A great many people and organizations helped in the creation of this memoir.

I could not have completed this book without Norman Mark, who helped to make this dream a reality and whose editing talents were most appreciated; Essee and Irv Kupcinet, who opened their home, files and memories to me while also sharing their many nostalgic photographs; the Pump Room for the use of many wonderful photos; John Reilly, who provided the wonderful photograph for the back cover; Rick Kogan, whose 1983 book "Sabers & Suites" revealed the true stories of Booth One and the Pump Room; Ann Gerber who gave good advice and provided many photographs; Richard Fegley of Playboy Magazine and Bill Zwecker, columnist for the Chicago Sun-Times, for their reminiscences and photographs; Lucia Adams for invaluable assistance in it's formative stages; Russell Lewis and the Chicago Historical Society for Chicago photographs; Fares Andrawes, manager of the Ambassador East Hotel, and Arthur Greenan, the manager of the Pump Room; Mary Cameron Frey, Linda Heister, and Fred Tokowitz, for their editorial consulting; Ray Fajmon and American Music World for the wonderful concert grand piano for the CD; Steven Maza transcription; Mary Lou Bilder Gold and the Sarah Siddons Society for photographs; the newspapers who opened their archives to me, including the Chicago Sun-Times, the Chicago Tribune and the Skyline Newspapers; Alva Johnston, whose three-part series on Ernie Byfield in the Saturday Evening Post provided important background material; and of course my collaborator, Diane Palmer, who spent over a year in exhaustive research, fact-checking, interviewing, writing and rewriting. Diane, without you this project could not have been completed.

A big, heartfelt thank you to all the celebrities who have shared their lives, triumphs and celebrations with me over the years. And most important, to all the people who danced and romanced to the music my orchestras have provided. Because of all of you, I thank my lucky stars every day.

Stanley Paul
Chicago, 1999

The following people shared their time, gave advice, revealed their memories and helped immensely with this book:

Gail Abraham
Audrey Adams
Irene Alexander
Ted Allen
Donna Beaumont Atwater
Hazel Barr
Nancy Berman
Marvin Berns
Beverly Blettner
Sherrill Bodine
Laurie Brady
Patricia Brickhouse
Margaret Carroll
Ed Chalfie
Winnie Chambers Clark
Cookie Cohen
Francie Comer
Terri D'Ancona
Mary Daniels
Aimee Devereux
Tom Doody
Mary Dougherty
Charlotte Doyle
Jerry Dukor
Ruth & Daniel Edelman
Siobhan Engle
Nina Feinberg
Dann Foley
Stella Foster
Loretta Foxgrover
June Travis Friedlob
Martin Gapshis
Evie Glieberman
Sondra Glog
Tiffani Kim Griffith
Helyn Goldenberg
Zarahda Gowenlock

Marilyn Hagnell
Nicki Harris
Angel Harvey
Mark Heister
Judy Hevrdejs
Ellie Himmel
Susan Holleb
Nena Ivon
Nancy Jennings
Sheila King
Van King
Nancy Klimley
Harriette Kretske
Michael Kutza
Donna LaPietra
George Lazerus
Joan Legittino
Johnny Legittino
Donald Levinson
Averill & Bernard Leviton
Steve Lombardo
Grace Mark
William J. McCluskey
Richard Melman
Helen Miller
Cindy Mitchell
Howard Mittelman
Patricia Moore
Robert Moreen
Daniel Nack
Jerry Norman
Cynthia Olson
Betty Orlandino
Jackie O'Brien
Maureen O'Mera
Potter Palmer
Jovana Papadokus

Alan Pearlman
Beverly Persky
Arturo Petterino
Bernice Pink
Sugar Rautbord
Myra Risher Reilly
Merle Reskin
Marilyn Resnick
Barbara Rinella
Tony Rossi
Shirley & Roy Schnakenberg
Emy Schwartz
Larry Selander
James Jennings Sheeran
Veronica & Phillip Siegal
Victor Skrebneski
Joyce Sloane
Steve Starr
John Sutton
Peggy Swift
Joyce Tanko
Darr & Ron Veltman
Eleanor Page Vosey
Mamie & Julius Walton
Carol Ware
Joan Wegner
Richard Weinberg
Joan Weinstein
Lois Weisberg
Nikki Weiss
James Wetzel
Abra Wilkin
Dori Wilson
Julie Wilson
Bess Winakor
Pat Wollman
Laura Zalloni

LINER NOTES

These songs are gifts from the composers to all of us. They are the medleys that I have enjoyed playing for many years.

While you are listening, imagine that you are back in the grand Pump Room in the Ambassador East Hotel in Chicago. A Famous Celebrity is sitting in Booth One. As friends are clustered nearby, a newsperson takes notes while a photographer records the moment, and you are there.

So, listen, relax . . . and then, if the rhythms cause a certain pleasant restlessness, grab a partner and dance:

1. "CHEEK TO CHEEK," from the RKO Radio Motion Picture "Top Hat," written by Irving Berlin in 1935.

> When you hear this song, you always think of the wonderful Fred Astaire. I had the opportunity to play it for him one evening as he walked into a party in his honor at the Ambassador Hotel. What a thrill it was.

2. Medley: "EASY TO LOVE" from the musical "Born To Dance," written by Cole Porter in 1936 and "ALL THE THINGS YOU ARE" from the musical "Very Warm For May" written by Oscar Hammerstein II and Jerome Kern in 1939.

> "Easy to Love" is one of my most favorite Cole Porter songs. I've coupled this with Jerome Kern's "All the Things You Are," which was almost cut from the Broadway opening of the musical "Very Warm for May." That would have been a mistake.

3. "CHANGE PARTNERS," from the RKO Radio Motion Picture "Carefree," written by: Irving Berlin in 1937.

> This was one of the songs that I played on my first night in the Pump Room. To this day, there are many nights when this is the song that gets the people on their feet to dance.

4. "IT'S DE-LOVELY," from the musical "Red, Hot And Blue!" written by: Cole Porter in 1936.

> This was a show-stopper on Broadway and it does the same for me almost nightly. Ethel Merman told me that Cole Porter kept on writing new verses to this song during the tryouts because people couldn't get enough of it.

5. "I COULD WRITE A BOOK" from "Pal Joey" written by Lorenz Hart and Richard Rodgers for the 1940 musical and also heard in the 1957 film starring Rita Hayworth, Frank Sinatra and Kim Novak.

Sinatra played Joey Evans, a cabaret singer who romances wealthy socialite Hayworth and sings this wonderful song to her.

6. Medley: "EMBRACEABLE YOU" and "BUT NOT FOR ME," both from the musical Production "Girl Crazy" written by: George Gershwin and Ira Gershwin in 1930. The 1943 movie starred Mickey Rooney and Judy Garland.

Both these gems were introduced by a 19-year-old Ginger Rogers at the Alvin Theater in New York in 1930.

I'll never forget one rainy afternoon in the mid '60s when Miss Rogers sat at my piano and taught me the little-known verse to "Embraceable You," which I've included here.

7. "RHODE ISLAND IS FAMOUS FOR YOU" written by Howard Dietz and Arthur Schwartz in 1948 for the Broadway show "Inside U.S.A."

Arthur Schwartz and lyricist Howard Dietz were a team that wrote many memorable tunes that have become classics. At one time, they were the height of song-writing sophistication.

On my way to my first job at the Piccolo Club in New York, I would stand outside the El Morocco nightclub to ogle the beautiful people. This song seemed to be wafting through the open doorway. It is one of the first obscure songs I learned in those early days in New York. Whenever I play it, I am reminded of a vanished, opulent, gentle era.

8. Medley: "WHERE OR WHEN" from "Babes In Arms" written by Richard Rodgers and Lorenz Hart in 1937 and "MY HEART STOOD STILL" from "A Connecticut Yankee" also written by Lorenz Hart and Richard Rodgers in 1927.

In 1919, when 16-year-old Richard Rodgers and 23-year-old Lorenz Hart began writing songs together, they shared a passion to elevate the craft of musical theater. They did.

We played this exact medley during my first big break at Basin Street East. Mr. Rodgers was in the audience, making that night even more thrilling.

9. "MAKE SOMEONE HAPPY" from the musical "Do Re Mi" written by Jule Styne in 1960.

This show opened soon after I arrived in New York and I fell in love with this song, which has become one of my all-time favorites.

10. Medley: "I GOT RHYTHM" from the musical "Girl Crazy" written by George Gershwin in 1930 and "SOMEBODY LOVES ME" from "George White's Scandals of 1924" also written by Gershwin.

We're performing this medley in the style of Arden & Ohman, the famous duo pianists of the 1920s.

"I Got Rhythm" is the Gershwin song that made a star out of a young girl, formerly known as Ethel Agnes Zimmerman, who stopped the show cold. That was Ethel Merman.

The musicians on this CD include:

Second piano—Ron Roetter

Bass—Bernie Hunter

Drums—Bob Berg

Crystall Recorders, February, 1999

Audio Engineer—Paul Wood

Mastered by Vince Micko

Produced by Stanley Paul

INDEX